A Warm and Gentle Welcome:
Nurturing Children from Birth to Age Three

THE GATEWAYS SERIES FIVE

Compiled from the work
of the WECAN RIE/Pikler Working Group

Editors: Trice Atchison and Margaret Ris
Managing Editor: Lory Widmer
Graphic Design: Sheila Harrington
WECAN Administrative Support: Melissa Lyons

© 2008 Waldorf Early Childhood Association of North America
First English Edition

RIE is a trademark of Resources for Infant Educarers.

Spacial Dynamics is a registered trademark of the Spacial Dynamics Institute, Inc.

Published in the United States by the Waldorf Early Childhood Association of North America
285 Hungry Hollow Road, Spring Valley, NY 10977

This publication is made possible through a grant from the Waldorf Curriculum Fund.

ISBN 978-0-9816159-3-6
10 9 8 7 6 5 4 3 2 1

Table of Contents

Foreword

by Susan Weber

We know that to birth an idea or initiative involves struggle, hard work and, ultimately, elation. This book, as a new creation, has traced a similar journey.

The writings included here on nurturing children from birth to age three reflect many years of study, colleagueship and practice. As Waldorf educators and caregivers strive to understand and meet the unique needs of children at this momentous stage of life, our work continues to deepen. Communities of colleagues—through sharing ideas, studies and practices—have, year by year, taken small steps forward. Threads have begun to weave a tapestry as colleagues continue to meet, and meet again—reconnecting with those who have crossed their paths over the years, but in new ways, with new questions and fresh insights.

Behind every earthly creation lies the world of spirit. As educators and caregivers have endeavored in the material world to understand how to most appropriately care for babies and toddlers, the spiritual world has drawn near to support those taking up this work, offering intuition and insight. Across continents from New Zealand, to Europe, to North and South America, a deep striving among educators has sparked a number of small initiatives dedicated to caring for our very youngest children with sensitivity, awareness and reverence. These initiatives, as they continue to grow, can be beacons of light for little children and their families in a world too often enshrouded in darkness.

We have learned much. We have found our way to insights and research offered by colleagues from other disciplines and streams, as well as by our own colleagues who are approaching the care of young children in light of the spiritual insights of Rudolf Steiner. We have looked at work relating to the phenomena of attachment and bonding, trauma and maternal depression, infant motor movement (particularly as seen through the eyes of Emmi Pikler), the unfolding of language, and practical aspects of caring for young children outside of their homes. We are learning a new language and building a new body of practice and study. It is heartening to find that the various streams often intersect, overlapping in remarkable and inspiring ways.

Innovative programs and approaches continue to emerge. I imagine that in twenty years we will look back and recognize that some have stood the test of time and that others have fallen away. And this is as it should be, for it is only out of our *doing* that insights can arise, out of the courage to try something. As the work unfolds, collegial sharing will remain the centerpiece to broadening our understanding. This is a tender undertaking that, like the infant herself, needs to be nurtured in order to grow.

Observe the young children around you; trust that you will find intuition from the heavens awaiting you as you enter the world of birth and earliest childhood.

∾

Introduction

by Trice Atchison and Margaret Ris

In recent years Waldorf early childhood educators have had to grapple with fundamental questions around the ever-increasing demand for out-of-home care and playgroups for very young children. They have asked themselves, "Can we take on this responsibility, knowing the sensitive nature of the young child?" Although Rudolf Steiner's indications for working with children and adolescents in Waldorf schools had been put to practical use for many decades, little existed on how best to meet the needs of children at the very beginning of life—particularly in light of societal trends such as daycare, single parenting, dual working families and the isolation of at-home mothers.

Out of the conviction that we are called upon to respond to the needs of the times, some individuals began to answer these questions with openness toward new initiatives for the future. These questions also began to receive attention on a worldwide scale, as evidenced by three international conferences in Switzerland and Sweden in the 1990s with the compelling theme, "The Dignity of the Young Child." The Medical Section of the Anthroposophical Society, together with the Waldorf/ Steiner Worldwide Initiative for Early Childhood Care, brought a much-needed focus on these earliest years of the child's life.

Also in the mid-1990s, several Waldorf educators from Antioch University New England, as part of a dialogue concerning the direction of the teacher training program there, engaged in conversation, study, travel, and observation. Their explorations included a visit to a center in Los Angeles called Resources for Infant Educarers, or RIE, founded by Magda Gerber, where they witnessed an approach to child care that was respectful, compelling and potentially supportive of work with the young child within Waldorf education circles. Although not outwardly working from a spiritual perspective, Gerber's approach appeared complementary to Waldorf early childhood education. She said, "The newborn baby…is between heaven and earth, not quite here yet…Trust that she will develop in her own time, rhythm and manner."[1]

RIE, they learned, was inspired by the work of Hungarian pediatrician Emmi Pikler, who founded the Pikler Institute in 1946, a children's home also commonly known as Lóczy. Delving deeper, they

---

1   Magda Gerber, *Your Self-Confident Baby: How to encourage your child's natural abilities—from the very start* (New York, NY: John Wiley and Sons, Inc., 1998), pp. 23-24.

learned that the Pikler Institute had a proven track record of research and publications showing how their principles and practices of sensitive caregiving led to long-term well-being in children reared there. Videos of the Pikler Institute's early work indicated to these educators that something of import and substance stood behind the scenes of graceful young children. Indeed, Pikler saw evidence of an innate wisdom at work during the first years of life, and cautioned against meeting babies' development with impatience, needless intervention, or hindrances. Her outlook echoed Rudolf Steiner's insight that "We accomplish significant steps in the early years of life. We work on ourselves in accordance with the highest wisdom...a wisdom that is more powerful and comprehensive than all the conscious wisdom we acquire later."[2]

On the East Coast, a cluster of Waldorf early childhood teachers began exploring what RIE could contribute to their work. A working group assembled, operating under the wings of WECAN, to find potential interrelationships among Waldorf education and RIE/Pikler principles. Reciprocally, on the West Coast, some pioneering RIE educators began to take an interest in Waldorf early childhood education.

Several members of the early WECAN working group were women in Waldorf-inspired, home-based daycare settings who sought new ways of relating to the children in their care. Others were teachers in established Waldorf schools who were charting new territory in caring for younger children and their parents. They wondered how to respond to colleagues' questions: "Isn't the best place for young children at home with their mothers?" Or, "For years we have insisted that children be three-and-a-half before entering a Waldorf nursery class—why are we caving in to societal pressure and possibly harming the children we seek to protect?" Gathering on a yearly basis, the group explored these and other themes, returned home to work with them, and reconvened to share ideas and insights. All were committed to bringing a new level of consciousness to their work with children.

In 2004 the Pikler Institute offered a new training program for English speaking participants. Nearly half of this first training group were Waldorf early childhood teachers, including members of the working group. The trainees came back full of insights and eager to share. More waves of Waldorf teachers made their way to Hungary, and interested colleagues and students gathered annually to continue exploring the question of how a RIE/Pikler approach might illuminate work with the young child. This volume—intended not as a definitive work, but rather as a continuing conversation—is in part the result of those meetings. It also includes several contributions from other Waldorf educators who have dedicated themselves to meeting the needs of infants and toddlers.[3]

"A Warm and Gentle Welcome," is a phrase that captures on many levels what is needed to support very young children. The articles included here emphasize how we can create an environment—both externally and within our hearts—that conveys to children that the world they

2   Rudolf Steiner, *The Spiritual Guidance of the Individual and Humanity* (Hudson, NY: Anthroposophic Press, 1991), pp. 8-9.

3   Because it is likely that many of the pieces in this book will be read and shared independently of the others, some repetition of information about RIE and the Pikler Institute has been retained. Readers are encouraged to refer to "Emmi Pikler's Trust in the Wise Infant" by Jane Swain for information about the origin and history of the Pikler Institute.

have just entered is indeed a welcoming place. In these pages we learn how slowing down enriches our caregiving, how a soothing voice and graceful gesture envelop the baby in a mantle of warmth and security, and how such exquisite, conscientious care honors the profound spiritual and bodily wisdom at work during the first years of life. We are given a picture of how, gradually, the child reaches out to the world—a world that expands daily as new experiences, abilities and relationships point the way to what it means to be human. We are encouraged to quietly observe children without an agenda and to give them, along with their parents, ample time and space to come into their own. It is our hope that this collection can serve as a resource and guide to accompany activity in the area of birth-to-three work as it continues to grow in depth and breadth. May these writings help you in your work of nurturing young children and their families.

Members of the WECAN working group over the years have included: Trice Atchison, Theresa Catlin, Joyce Gallardo, Monica Gallardo, Andrea Gambardella, Joan Kahn, Vanessa Mitchell Kohlhaas, Kim Lewis, Nancy Macalaster, Marilyn Pelrine, Margaret Ris, Theresa deJesus Savel, Jane Swain, Mary Truilisi, and Susan Weber.

Some individuals at the forefront of exploring the interrelationships among Waldorf, RIE and Pikler approaches to caring for young children include, on the East Coast, Rena Osmer, Ann Pratt and Susan Weber, among others. On the West Coast, longtime RIE educator Hari Grebler completed her Waldorf early childhood training and began integrating the two streams in her work. We are grateful to the many other Waldorf/Steiner educators in North America and around the world who have also been charting new territory in working with our youngest children.

The Changing Needs of the Family— The Fundamental Needs of the Child

Meeting the Needs of the Times

by Cynthia K. Aldinger

This article previously appeared in What Is A Waldorf Kindergarten, *published by Steiner Books in 2007, and in WECAN's Gateways newsletter (Issue 52, Spring/Summer 2007). It offers a brief overview of the expansion of the Waldorf/Steiner early childhood movement in North America to include parent-tot and parent-infant programs, extended day programs and child care. It is within this expansion toward the younger child that Waldorf/Steiner educators became more aware of the work of Emmi Pikler and Magda Gerber. This chapter also introduces the work of LifeWays North America, which promotes a Steiner-based approach to home-like childcare and honors Emmi Pikler's research on the importance of the caregiver-child relationship and the allowance of self-directed movement in infants and toddlers.*

Rudolf Steiner believed that one of the essential aspects of education was to teach in such a way that the children would learn how to properly breathe. In early childhood we might say "to live in such a way that the children will learn how to breathe."

As a young child in the 1950s, when my mother worked part-time I was always with my grandparents. On days my mother did not work, I was home—all day—several days in a row. Occasionally, mother would go to a neighbor's home for coffee and a chat, and I would go with her and play with the children of that household. Whether I was at grandma's house or at home, I was playing by myself or with neighborhood children while the adults went about tending the home. Often my mother would gather the neighborhood children together and sing with us and read stories. It was not called "home-based preschool" back then. It was just life, like breathing.

Thirty years later, when I was teaching in a mixed-age Waldorf kindergarten, it was a joy to create the flow of activities—time for active robust play and for quiet listening, for being together in a group or skipping away with a best friend, for cleaning and caring, for baking and eating, time to create useful and beautiful things and time to dig in the sand. The daily, weekly and seasonal rhythms were like breathing in and out.

The Waldorf kindergarten was, and is, a place that honors childhood. In my experience, it was even more. It was a haven. As a founding teacher, there was always more to deal with than just the parents and children of my own kindergarten. There were faculty meetings, college meetings, board meetings, festival committee meetings, long-range planning meetings, and so on. Going out into the school to attend to such things was like venturing out into the world. Returning to my kindergarten was like "coming home." Elementary school colleagues would occasionally come into my kindergarten in the afternoon to rest while their children were with another teacher. The couch was there to welcome them.

The kindergarten was not a classroom. It was a child's play garden. Over the years as the kindergarten became more and more permeated with our routines and rituals, our ebbs and flows, our joys and sorrows, our work and play, the room became like a silent pedagogue, the walls embracing us like a benevolent grandmother who sees all but knows when to turn her head to allow just the right measure of mischief. I remember those joyful occasions when I would step out of the room just before clean up time was finished, knowing the pure delight it provided the children to "barricade" the door while they completed the final details of putting things away. When the children opened the door, I would walk back in, not as the teacher, but as the village inspector to a chorus of giggles as I noticed all the marvelous detail that had gone into the tidying away. We were our own little community, and even when I was a younger teacher, I felt like the beloved grandmother or auntie who welcomed the neighborhood children over to play for a few hours in the morning. At the end of the morning, the children left with their parents or caregivers to go home or to visit with friends.

Over time some things began to change. Children who had been in traditional institutional child care since infancy were beginning to come into the kindergarten. Many of them did not understand how to enter into self-directed imaginative play. Other children came who had not been in child care but had been enrolled in multiple enrichment programs since toddlerhood. Many children also needed care beyond the kindergarten morning. Some families requested this extension because both parents needed to work in order to afford tuition for a Waldorf/Steiner School. Others simply felt that their children thrived in the longer day with other children rather than at home. The reasons for wanting the longer hours varied, but the requests were strong. Also, more families with children younger than three emphatically asked, "What programs do you have for my child?" They made it clear that, while Waldorf/Steiner education was their first choice, if our schools could not serve their needs, they would go elsewhere.

Parents were seeking "more" for their children—more hours, more years in school, more activities, more time away from home. In this age of individualized loneliness, parents were also seeking community and were asking for guidance on how to be with their children.

How were we, as Waldorf Schools, going to meet these needs?

Schools began offering extended days. Children who needed the extended day would gather from all of the early childhood programs and have lunch together, followed by rest time, then a light snack and a bit more play time before being picked up. Some schools included lunch as part of the kindergartens and then dismissed the children to After Care or to go home. Typically the early childhood After Care program ended when the elementary school day ended around 3 p.m. Children who needed even later care would go to another After Care program until 5 or 6 p.m. This continues to be the pattern for many schools. Others are beginning to offer full-day kindergartens to avoid so much switching around for the children.

To respond to parents' requests to serve younger children, many schools began offering "nursery" or "pre-school" programs for children just under three to a little over four. Some even began accepting a few two-year-olds. At my school it was called the Wonder Garden, and I remember the wise insights of its first teacher Laura Cassidy when she noted that it simply did not work to have a "pressed down" kindergarten morning for these little ones. She noted how much slower the pace needed to be with only little ones present and no older children there to help or model for them. She recognized that bodily care, dressing and undressing, toileting, and such were valid and important parts of their daily experience and needed to be given plenty of time.

Schools also began offering programs to stem the tide of loneliness of the parents and to bring in even younger children. Called parent-child programs or playgroups, these programs were usually one morning a week for a couple of hours. In some schools, parent-infant or parent-toddler programs were also offered. They have become so popular that several groups convene throughout the week. Many schools have begun to see them as enrollment builders, although many teachers view them primarily as support for parents. They want to strengthen the healthy development of families regardless of whether the families later enroll in their schools. Typically, many families do enroll in the school because they have been inspired by their experience in the parent-child programs.

These expanding programs that kept the children at the school longer hours and brought children out of their homes at younger and younger ages were not always welcomed into our Waldorf/Steiner early childhood movement. In some schools there was excitement about this development. Others treaded forward with trepidation. Still others chose not to have young children in any school program other than the kindergartens. Why the resistance? Let us consider the following statement by Rudolf Steiner regarding the child in the first three years:

> *The first two-and-a-half years are the most important of all…During this time the child has the gift of being instinctively aware of everything that goes on around it, especially as regards the people who come in daily contact with it…Everything that takes place in its environment imprints itself on its physical bodily form…so that our behavior will influence its disposition to health or disease for the whole of its after life.*[1]

---

[1] Rudolf Steiner, *Understanding Young Children: Excerpts from Lectures by Rudolf Steiner Compiled for the Use of Kindergarten Teachers* (Silver Spring, MD: Waldorf Kindergarten Association, 1994), p. 2. From "The Child Before the Seventh Year," lecture series given in Dornach, December 23 1921 - January 7, 1922.

Dr. Steiner speaks of the first three years of life with great reverence. He impels us to understand the depth of responsibility we take on when in the presence of these little ones so recently arrived from the realms of spirit. As poet William Wordsworth wrote in his poem "Ode: Intimations of Immortality," "trailing clouds of glory do we come from God who is our home." Our movement has a very protective gesture toward this early period of life, holding as an ideal the image of the child at home, cared for by a loving family. To open programs for children under three-and-a-half, even though accompanied by their parents, was a big step for us to take.

Yet the phenomenon of playgroups was becoming a cultural norm. If we did not provide these opportunities, parents would find them elsewhere. Many schools decided it would be wise to support families who were seeking not only community with other parents but also guidance about raising their children. Today parent-child teachers are grateful to meet these families who, regardless of lifestyle and parenting practices, have found their way to our schools. Every parent-child teacher can share testimonials of how the program has helped families make life-changing choices for their homes.

Now, let us consider the resistance to extending the school day for kindergarten children. Again, there was a long-held belief that the best place for young children was the home. The hope was that after a morning in the kindergarten, the children would go home and have lunch followed by a nap, then an afternoon of play. What has been happening for years, however, in North America, is that children who were being picked up after kindergarten were not necessarily going home. Perhaps they were going out to lunch and then to run errands or to attend a variety of "enrichment" classes such as ballet, music, gymnastics, or sports. Partly for this reason, some schools began adding lunch to the end of the kindergarten morning. Others began experimenting with extended day programs. It was a new dimension of our work, and we did not necessarily know how best to go about it.

At my school our first attempt at offering an extended day for the kindergarten children resulted in cranky, tired children coming to school the next day after they attended After Care. Over the years and with dedicated intention on the part of those carrying the afternoon program, things improved. We changed the name from After Care to TLC (Tender Loving Care) and consciousness was given to how the transition took place from the kindergarten morning to the afternoon. The kindergarten teachers worked with the TLC teachers to build a conscious bridge of care and loving exchange. Currently most schools offer some type of extended day for their early childhood children.

Today a common experience in our schools is as follows: a child as young as an infant or toddler comes to school with a parent or caregiver to attend a parent-child program for a few years, followed by attending a nursery or pre-school program for a year or two, followed by attending a kindergarten program, and often spending the afternoons with different teachers in an extended day program. Some children experience two extended day programs because the program for young children ends at 3:00 or so, and then they switch to the "after school" program that goes to 5 or 6 p.m. In the course of a day, they may have been with three different sets of teachers. The good news is that the children do not have to travel to a whole different school or day care program in the afternoons.

However, for many Steiner/Waldorf early childhood educators this is not the type of schedule they desire for young children. Consider this quotation from Rudolf Steiner in the book *The Child's Changing Consciousness*: "The task of the kindergarten teacher is to adjust work taken from daily life so that it becomes suitable for the children's play activities… Whatever a young child is told to do should not be artificially contrived by adults who are comfortable in our intellectual culture, but should spring from life's ordinary tasks. The whole point of a nursery class is to give young children the opportunity to imitate life in a simple and wholesome way."[2]

Taking into account the current *culture of adult life* in the Western world with its busyness, its days filled with a variety of activities and comings and goings and restlessness, this model of shifting the children from one setting to the next throughout the day is very contemporary. But is it the lifestyle we want them to imitate when they are so young? Does it allow the space and time for them to penetrate their play? Does it meet the fundamental needs of the young child?

In *The Essentials of Education* Dr. Steiner said, "For the small child before the change of teeth, the most important thing in education is the teacher's own being."[3] Compare this to what contemporary pediatrician Dr. T. Berry Brazelton says in his book *The Irreducible Needs of Children*: "Supportive, warm, nurturing emotional interactions with infants and young children…help the central nervous system grow appropriately."[4] While young children may exhibit amazing levels of resiliency, are we best serving their needs by shifting their environment and their teachers/caregivers so frequently?

In the mid-nineties, the Waldorf Kindergarten Association noticed that many teachers had begun caring for children in their homes, some for personal reasons and others because they felt that they could better provide the type of seamless day and rhythmical flow in which young children thrive. At the East Coast Waldorf Kindergarten conference in 1996 one of the workshops was specifically for individuals offering child care in homes or centers. Many who attended spoke with tender vulnerability of their sense of being viewed as "wrong" to offer care for infants and toddlers or to offer care for long days. They experienced a pervasive feeling that this was not the Waldorf way and that children needed to be at home before the kindergarten years and needed to go back home each day after kindergarten.

Rather than being criticized for their efforts, the people attending the workshop were thanked for taking the courageous step of trying to meet the needs of the times. Not long after that, the Waldorf Kindergarten Association changed its name to the Waldorf Early Childhood Association of North America (WECAN), sending a clear message that they were not only an association of teachers in kindergartens but also included colleagues in a variety of other venues.

2   Rudolf Steiner, *The Child's Changing Consciousness* and Waldorf Education (Hudson, NY: Anthroposophic Press, 1988), p. 81. From a lecture given on April 18, 1923.

3   Rudolf Steiner, *The Essentials of Education* (Hudson, NY: Anthroposophic Press, 1991), p. 14.

4   T. Berry Brazelton and Stanley Greenspan, *The Irreducible Needs of Children: What Every Child Must Have to Grow, Learn, and Flourish* (New York: Da Capo, 2001), p. 1.

Around this same time, Rena Osmer and I, both WECAN board members, began traveling and visiting traditional childcare centers in the U.S. and studying the changes that were taking place in home life. There had been a paradigm shift regarding the daily life of the young child. Fifty years ago, the home was typically the place where the children played and learned about daily life, and the kindergarten was where parents sent them for artistic and playful enrichment for a couple of hours in the morning. The parental home was still the place where children experienced the main thrust of domestic life. Currently in our culture, parents are drawn to taking their children out of the home for increased stimuli. The activities of "housekeeping" or "homemaking" are sometimes relegated to being done when the children are not at home or when they are sleeping. As will be mentioned later, the daily life experiences of what makes a household function are becoming less and less common for children.

Rena and I became convinced that it was time for Steiner-based child care and support for parents to grow and be strengthened in North America. With respect toward those who had already begun to work in these arenas and with an interest in expanding even further, we explored the question of what we thought Steiner-based child care would ideally look like. Our conclusion was that it would be imitative of the qualities and activities found in healthy, rhythmical home life—the ways of life. Thus came the name LifeWays, which we adapted from our friends who wrote the first *Lifeways* books.[5] By 1998, the first LifeWays Child Care Center was opened in rural southeast Wisconsin and several others have opened since.

LifeWays centers and homes are designed to feel like home-away-from-home. Too often the missing ingredients in traditional childcare settings are consistency, warmth, and long-lasting relationships. The heart of LifeWays childcare is the "Family Suite" in which children, caregivers, and families develop long-term relationships in an environment that protects childhood and enhances optimal physical, socio-emotional, cognitive and spiritual health for the children and the caregivers. What ages the various sites care for and how long their days run vary from place to place. There is not one defined model.

The Milwaukee LifeWays Child Development Center has three suites with a full range of ages from infant to six-year-olds. The center offers care from 7:30 a.m. to 5:30 p.m. Some caregivers choose to work for eight hours a day while others prefer to share a suite and work part-time. Set up to imitate a large family, each suite has seven to eight children with a primary caregiver. With three suites, the center functions like a small neighborhood or extended family. All the children get to know all the caregivers, and they have a special connection to their primary caregivers. The caregivers are supported by a part-time director (who is also the parent-child teacher), other part-time caregivers, a cook, a kindergarten teacher, and volunteers. The older children of the suites may attend the preschool or the forest kindergarten two or three mornings a week and are sometimes joined by community children who come only for the preschool or kindergarten. During this time, the youngest children in the suites have a quiet time with their caregivers, similar to how it is at home when older siblings go off to school for a while. When the older children return to the suite, the infants and toddlers are delighted to see them.

---

5   Gudrun Davy and Bons Voors, eds. *Lifeways: Working with Family Questions* (Stroud, UK: Hawthorn Press, 1983).

In addition to LifeWays centers, there are individuals who offer LifeWays child care and/or preschool in their homes. In many ways this is ideal. They are already in a home, so they don't have to imitate being in a home. Trisha Lambert, who was a "Full" WECAN member and a LifeWays "Representative," was a Waldorf Kindergarten teacher in a school before deciding to offer care at her home. She was doing this already before the LifeWays organization began. Initially inspired by Helle Heckmann in Denmark, Trisha and the children would spend a long time outside each day exploring the numerous gardens and grounds surrounding her home. She prepared meals and snacks for the children, and they slept in the living room and bedroom of her home. Most days they had a little time for some simple circle games and a story, and if there was a baby in the mix, the baby played or slept while the other children sang and played. Like the Milwaukee LifeWays Center, Trisha had an ongoing waiting list. Many families can feel that the simplicity of daily living offered in these settings is what best serves their children, and often wonderful stories emerge of how families begin to slowly transform their own homes to be more reflective of the practices they have observed.

The rhythms and activities of the days and weeks in a LifeWays setting are meant to imitate home life rather than school life—daily care and cleaning of the environment, bodily care of the children, doing laundry, putting away groceries, eating, sleeping, singing and playing, crafting for special seasonal activities. While the cook prepares the organic lunch each day, the caregivers and children in each suite participate throughout the week in the preparation of the food—for example, peeling carrots, chopping onions, and so on. Whether or not the children actively participate in the work being done, they thrive within the environment of the focused work of their caregivers.

Called "The Living Arts" (domestic, nurturing, creative and social), these daily life activities are quietly disappearing from the routine experience of many children today. In full-day care it is easier to experience a natural flow of these activities without feeling hurried. One notices that the children have more time to penetrate such things as putting on their shoes, brushing their teeth, having their hair brushed, getting dressed to go outside, watching a baby being fed or diapered. The breath of the mid-day sleep also helps. Whether or not the caregiver also sleeps, there is a natural shift that takes place that allows for a qualitatively different experience from morning to afternoon. When they awaken from nap and have their hair brushed and faces oiled (a practice adopted from Bernadette Raichle's Awhina child care center in New Zealand), they are ready for the slower pace of afternoon play and getting ready to go home.

The caregivers attend a mentor-supported, one-year, part-time LifeWays training that introduces them to the Living Arts as well as to the LifeWays principles and suggested practices. Human development is taught from the spiritual scientific insights of Rudolf Steiner and contemporary child development experts. Students experience music, movement and speech classes to strengthen them as human beings worthy of being imitated by young children and are offered numerous handwork classes, including an introduction to gardening, to steep them in the practical, yet aesthetic, craft of homemaking. Other parts of the training focus on working with regulatory agencies as well as how to work with parents and colleagues. A unique aspect of the LifeWays training is that the students include parents, childcare providers, nannies, home-based preschool teachers, parent-child educators, and grandparents. The common denominator is the understanding that the fundamental needs of young children can be met through the life activity of the home regardless of whether you are a stay-at-home parent or a child care provider or a parent educator.

Just as it was a privilege to teach in a Waldorf kindergarten so many years ago, it is an equal privilege to be a part of the ongoing development of Steiner-inspired child care. While going back in time is not the answer, many Waldorf/Steiner early childhood educators have discovered the value of slowing down, shifting the emphasis to daily life activities, and expanding their time with children in their care. LifeWays is one part of this expanded work of Waldorf/Steiner educators. There are others who have been offering child care for two decades or longer, and still others offering training and support for parent-child teachers and teachers who wish to be involved with birth-to-three work.

At the Waldorf early childhood conference in New York in 2006, the keynote speaker was Dr. Michaela Glöckler, director of the medical section at the Goetheanum. Susan Silverio, director of the Northeast LifeWays training, shared her notes quoting Dr. Glöckler as follows: "Teach beyond guilt. Teach out of Joy! Open up [early childhood programs] outside of the school landscape! Organize farming/play afternoons in family homes." By responding to the genuine needs of our times in these and other creative ways, we can best support and nurture parents and children.

We are pleased to be involved with this expanded consciousness around early childhood practices and family support, and we are grateful to the Waldorf Early Childhood Association of North America for having the foresight and warmth of heart to support individuals and organizations which are furthering the work. It is a breath of fresh air.

∽◦∽

Cynthia Aldinger is founder and executive director of LifeWays North America, an organization dedicated to the development of healthy childcare and parenting practices. She founded the first LifeWays Child Care Center in 1997 in Wisconsin, USA, and now directs LifeWays trainings and seminars across the United States and also lectures and presents internationally and throughout North America. She is an adjunct faculty member at Rudolf Steiner College, California, serves on the board of the Waldorf Early Childhood Association of North America, and is a member of the National Association for the Education of Young Children and a supporter of the Alliance for Childhood. Aldinger was the founding teacher for Prairie Hill Waldorf School in Wisconsin, now in its 21st year. She received her teaching certificate from Emerson College in Sussex, England. Her passion is the preservation of the playful spirit of childhood and helping to create home-like environments that provide the comfort, security and activities found in a healthy home. Aldinger has been married for thirty-five years and is the mother of two adult sons.

Do We Know Why We Do What We Do?
An Interview with Helle Heckmann

by Margaret Ris

Last summer in Boston, I had the opportunity to speak with Waldorf early childhood educator Helle Heckmann. Helle is founder and director of Nøkken, a Waldorf daycare center in Denmark for children ages one through seven that has served as an inspiration to Waldorf kindergartens and nurseries worldwide. She had recently completed a three-month tour of Waldorf early childhood programs throughout North America. Here Helle shares some of her insights on the evolving needs of children and families in today's culture, particularly in regard to the needs of the youngest children in daycare and early childhood environments.

MR: Helle, what have you seen in these past fifteen years or so since you started Nøkken regarding the evolution of care for very young children from a Waldorf perspective?

HH: I've seen that the need for care of young children has exploded from when I visited the United States eleven years ago. Now things are very different and we need to ask, "How do we approach our task in order to best meet the needs of the youngest children?"

MR: What are your biggest concerns?

HH: This heightened demand for childcare gives rise to many different approaches. You cannot make one model for the little child—there are many different needs. Some children need care for short periods of time, some for longer days. Mothers also must find their way. Mothers often need to work, but they still need to make caring for their children a priority. Certain mothers in the States can still stay home; many fewer in Europe can *[beyond the national allowance for maternity leave, generally six to twelve months, depending on the country]*.

My biggest concern regarding caring for little children is that most initiatives are splitting up children by ages and children are placed exclusively with their own age group. The children can only mirror themselves, so they become dependent on adults in learning how to approach the world. This can be good in some ways; the adult is the role model for food preparation and cleaning, for example. But to play and become social, for that you need a wider age range of children.

One- and two-year-olds mostly watch; without bigger children to observe, they don't really learn to play. Many conflicts occur in same-age groups. For me, to have mixed ages creates the feeling of an old-fashioned family. This is important because many children today are "only children," or there is a large age span between children in the family. If these children are to learn how to give care, they need to see care being given. This is also true for the bigger children—they need to see care being given so that they have experience to draw upon when they become parents. The bigger children can measure where they have come from when they are around little ones, and the younger children get an idea of where they are going and how to approach life.

MR: Can you comment on any changes you've noticed in the way children play?

HH: In play today all around the world, I can see that many children do not "play house" with mother, father and child. These days the modern family is often a composite—children don't see much caregiving, so they can't imitate it in their play. They seem more often to play at caring for pets— buying food, speaking to the animals, being nice to them—than at caring for children. We need to bring back doll play; children need to be around adults actively engaged in caregiving activities so that the children can learn by seeing the actual doing, not by the intellectual telling of it.

MR: What sorts of activities do you wish children had more, or less, of?

HH: The whole process of caring for the little child matters. For instance, with changing diapers, so few use cloth, but instead use the highly effective diapers that eliminate smells. These diapers can be left on for five or six hours, rather than two hours, so now diapering time, that "You-and-I," intimate, private time when one talks or sings to the child, is much reduced. During these intimate moments, children can experience the feeling, "I am seen, I am loved." When this happens, mother, too feels she has been with the child and can then leave her to play on her own for a little while.

The intimacy of eating time is also challenged today. While breastfeeding, the mother often reads, watches TV or talks on the phone. Those who bottle-feed may give the child a bottle while he's strapped into a stroller. In both cases, there's no relationship.

So the natural, intimate, nourishing situations of being together have been compromised.

Today more and more children have difficulties with the sense of touch, because they are exposed to the world so early, rather than given more private and intimate time with the caregiver. You see the youngest babies in strollers that face out toward the world, rather than back toward the parent. The baby experiences, "Where is my center? Do I know where I am in the world?" Even in infant carriers, when the baby is placed facing outward, just hanging there, we steer them away from an intimate connection and expose them to the world before they are ready.

MR: How do you think we can best reach mothers?

HH: As professional caregivers, we have knowledge of how the child develops physically and also mentally. By being role models in our initiatives, we can inspire mothers to put the question to themselves, "How can I best care for my child?"

When parents have little children, they are very open to inspiration, because many parents of today have so little background in parenting. As a result, they are searching out there in the world for guidance on how to care for their child. All parents wish the best for their children. There are thousands of books to buy, but that's intellectual information. There is little in the way of "doing," of being shown how to do it.

MR: What are some of the special considerations you'd like parents and caregivers to keep in mind about the very youngest children?

HH: Little children are not little adults. They are very special. Children under three are not small kindergarteners. They need a lot of time to observe their world—then, in imitation, to be one with the world. It is so important that those who care for the child know how much they affect the child. They need to be very aware of themselves as role models—not only in their doing, but in being a moral and spiritual person. Those who work with little children should actually be the most spiritually developed persons.

The little child feels everything the adult contains. The child imitates the movement, and also the mood. If there is not a correspondence between what you say and what you do, the child gets confused. Today people too often say what they don't want the child to do; but what does the adult mean? And what, then, should the child do? If the child is very often exposed to a disharmony between what the adult herself says and what she does, the child can read the body language and see the incongruity. This can create difficulties for the child in building trust in the adult.

MR: Can you talk about the balance between speaking and silence when in the presence of young children?

HH: Even though the little child learns to speak from listening to language, it is actually quite important to be silent around young children. When we do speak, it is important not to use baby language or approach the child as if she is an imbecile. Rather, we can use short sentences with clear language.

As the adult, we make the decision and then clearly tell the child what we wish her to do. Know that you are the decision maker. The child is not your friend; she is your responsibility.

MR: Can Waldorf schools responsibly add care of children less than three years of age to their offerings?

HH: First, I think we must remove the word school from the English language when it comes to working with children under the age of seven—and use instead the terms "homes" or "gardens for children." Since the children are spending so much time away from home, they need, more then ever before, a homely environment where all the basic activities of a home are carried out. Otherwise, children cannot learn how to take care of their environment.

In the past, children no younger than four went to kindergartens to engage in social and artistic activities for a few hours a day. Now many children much younger than four spend more time in the kindergarten or in childcare than at home during their waking hours. This means that there are completely new demands on our work, and we have to recognize that we must adjust to meet these demands. So much is different today, and the family structure has shifted dramatically. We are fully capable of creating a good environment for children from ages one to seven. But we need to be willing to change how we build up the daily life of our children's gardens, because the ages of the children we care for, and the hours they are in our care, have changed.

MR: What do you see as crucial to the care of children?

HH: One of the main goals and needs of the little child is to learn how to get a rhythm in life. Children also need proper movement, meaning that they must spend time out-of-doors, which can offer many more challenges than the indoor environment. Children also need to sleep, to learn how to let go and trust themselves to fall into a healthy sleep. Many, many children today get far too little sleep because they are treated as little adults—and yet the children learn and grow most when they are asleep. Good sleep is necessary to their healthy development.

Nutrition is an important issue. Many children today have problems with eating. They struggle with how to eat, how to be social, wait, sit while everybody is served, listen, chew with a closed mouth, eat with a spoon or fork, and also how to be nourished. Many children are picky eaters. If we sit together to eat the same food, out of imitation many will learn proper eating. Because the adult knows what is best for the child, she chooses the foods.

Rhythm, movement, sleep, eating and caregiving—all of these are central. Caregiving includes proper dressing for outdoor and indoor life according to the environment, whether the child be in the sandbox, outside in the rain (dressed in rain trousers), or in the cold (dressed warmly). When the child senses that he is valued enough for someone to take care of him as a person—brush his hair, put on a sunhat, or bundle up—all of this together supports a healthy self-esteem. The child then is freer to explore the world in a way that is safe.

MR: What else do you see as essential for the young child?

HH: Children in caregiving environments have the opportunity to develop social skills, which is essential because without social skills we will be very, very lonesome. They can learn only by being together with others—not in front of a TV or computer or by being told *how* to behave. By doing things and being together socially in an authentic way, children can learn what life is.

So, our Waldorf initiatives have to be places where real life is being lived and the basic tasks of life are visible. This way, the children can learn how to be a part of life and that they are needed—not just attached, but truly a part of what's going on.

MR: What about the idea that we're in the age of the Individual? How do you foster the individuality of a child?

HH: There is no doubt that we are very special individuals, every one of us. Each individual has to be approached where he or she is in life. The caregiver has to be able to see the different needs of each unique child, and to offer possibilities or challenges that meet the child where he or she is developmentally at a given point in time.

This means that the caregiver has to have wide-ranging knowledge about what possibilities can be offered to children, particularly those who may have challenges and difficulties.

MR: How do we approach the child in these special cases?

It can be a challenge to approach the child with the right attitude, so that he is free to follow his own way. For example, when a child doesn't crawl, I can place a tree stump in its path so that the child *has* to crawl over. I cannot make a child crawl. But I can create the environment that encourages crawling as a response. I cannot help a child climb a tree, but I can give her a chance to meet a tree that she can choose to climb or not. I will not help the child to climb. If they see other children climbing they may become inspired, but some still will not climb and I have to accept that.

I see myself as walking alongside the child, not in front or behind. I offer opportunity, but it is the child who has to take it. This is very individual, whether and how a child will accept a challenge. It is important that I do not force the child to be who I expect him to be, but that I accept him for who he is.

MR: Can you speak a bit more about differences?

HH: In carrying a picture of how the child should be, we can sometimes forget to see that a certain child has a way to be that's different. We can provide opportunities that challenge the child in healthy ways, and from our modeling show how to approach other people with respect. It's important for all the children that we structure the day and keep in mind the boundaries and social expectations for the group. Through role modeling and rhythm, the children can see plainly what is expected of other human beings. Yet within that, there is freedom for the individual to develop as he or she is.

MR: When you say that the child from birth to age three is not just a little kindergartener, how might you work with a teacher to adjust her approach?

HH: I would have her make observations of little children for a couple of weeks, because when you teach yourself how to observe, you also realize how different the very youngest children are, how much time they need, how very silent they are, and how very serious. You notice how important it is for them to have structure around them, for you to repeat everything over and over again, and that you are faithful to the rhythm of the day. You see also that you must be quiet, and never surprise them or stress them. With little children, you never tell them what to do with your words, but with your actions, your doing.

You realize that with very young children you should not do storytelling or activities such as beeswax modeling and painting, but instead should clean, iron, make food, and sing. You recognize that they need to see you visibly doing activities, and so you make sure the children can see you and imitate you. You realize, too, that you must move slowly and purposefully, and that the children need to know that, despite your activity, you are always available. All of this is so different from the kindergarten-aged child, who can be inspired in a completely different way through storytelling, long circle games and festival activities. There are two different sets of needs.

The little ones can be part of a kindergarten but should not participate in the kindergarten activities. They need much more quiet eating and sleeping times, so it might be good to separate the two groups at times, allowing the little ones to eat and sleep together aside from the older ones. But in general in the kindergarten it would be good to leave it so that the children do not all have to do everything at the same time. It can be controlling: "Now you all paint together, now you do beeswax," etc. The most important thing, in any case, is to ask ourselves, *Why?* We need to know *why* we want to do something and then we find *how* to do it. In this way we are open and responsive to the real needs of the children in our care.

MR: You've seen childcare in many countries. Being both a realist and a visionary, what would you recommend as a national policy towards maternity/paternity leave that would give ample consideration to the needs of parents in the workforce and their young children?

HH: I think it should be a right to stay home during the first year of childhood because this time is so special and the foundation for the mother-child bond is laid. It takes time to get to know your child. Development through the first year of life goes so quickly and every day new capacities unfold. For the family to grow together, it is important for them to have the time together to observe these remarkable changes.

To become upright in the world is a gift, and to grow in safe and secure surroundings is necessary. Of course, we have to support mothers in this period so they do not feel alone. We need to offer courses and help them learn to observe their baby's development and to counter the loneliness they can feel being at home by themselves with only a baby as company. We need to facilitate the formation of mothers' groups so that mothers can support each other and grow together with their children.

MR: Is there anything else you feel is important to share with teachers and childcare professionals who are taking on this pioneering work?

HH: My advice would be to slow down. What is it that we are in such a hurry *for*? The greatest truths reside in the smallest of details; macrocosms dwell in microcosms. Everything happens where we are—we just need to see it. Life is a challenge and we need to see it as something we are part of and understand that how we meet our challenges matters. When we do this, we can recognize that we are giving our children an image of how adults meet life situations. This picture is something children will be able to gain inspiration from in the future.

The Developing Child
in the
First Three Years

Emmi Pikler's Trust in the Wise Infant

by Jane Swain

The Pikler Institute—often called Lóczy (pronounced Loh-tsee) after the street where it is located in Budapest, Hungary—was originally built in 1946 as an orphanage for children ages birth to three whose parents were killed in World War II or were in tuberculosis asylums. In continuous operation since it was founded by pediatrician Emmi Pikler, Lóczy today cares for children up to six years old, most of whom have been abused, neglected or abandoned, and a few of whom have special needs. More recently, the institute began offering parent-child classes and a daycare program. It also serves as a training and observation center that draws participants from around the world who wish to learn more about Lóczy's renowned practices that support the healthy development of children. At the core of the institute's philosophy is an understanding of the need to provide an environment in which children are nurtured, respected, and allowed freedom of movement so that they may grow and develop in security, relationship to others, and self-mastery.

In June 2007, I took a two-week course for professionals who work with young children, and also had the opportunity to observe in the orphanage. During the first week of the course we studied gross motor and fine motor development, along with their relationship to cognitive development and attention. During week two we studied the attentive, caring activity of the adult.

Before I went to Budapest, I had read about Emmi Pikler's remarkable contributions, and had worked with colleagues who had repeatedly visited Lóczy; I thought I was well-informed. But in Budapest, there was so much more to learn. My purpose in writing this article is first to explain the basic philosophy of the Pikler Institute and then to share some of my insights and relate them to my experiences as a pediatric physical therapist with training in sensory integration,[1] neurodevelopmental treatment,[2] and Spacial Dynamics.[3]

---

1   Sensory integration was originated by A. Jean Ayres and refers to the neurological process of taking in information through the senses, organizing it, and using it to function in daily life.

2   Neurodevelopmental treatment was originated by Berta and Karel Bobath and is a treatment approach for children and adults with neurological challenges such as cerebral palsy and strokes.

3   Spacial Dynamics was originated by Jaimen McMillan and is a discipline involving spatially oriented movement exercises, games, observations and therapeutics.

Pikler's theories grew out of observation

Emmi Pikler (1902-1984) was a pediatrician with exceptional observational abilities. Early in her career, she and her husband lived in Triest, Italy, for a year. There she spent time on the beach observing parents with their infants. Her observations showed her the tremendous importance of the parents' love for their child. Pikler also witnessed parents "teaching" their infants to sit, stand and walk before they were able to do so on their own, causing the infants to do something different than they would have if left to their own initiative.

Pikler saw this gesture of the adult as a distrust of the child's abilities. She believed that children have an innate capacity to direct the unfolding of their motor capacities through self-initiated movement, if given the time and space to do so, and she based her practices on this idea. Pikler also believed that each child was qualified for this task—in fact, infinitely more qualified than any adult. It follows, then, that infants should not be taught motor skills, but instead should be allowed gradually to come into the vertical positions of sitting and standing entirely through their own efforts.

The relationship between the infant and primary adult

Pikler saw the infant's ability to self-initiate movement as a function of the security of the relationship with the primary adult. This is a concept generally lacking in therapeutic practices in this country. At Lóczy, each child has one of his nurses, as the caregivers are called, designated as his primary nurse. The primary nurse knows the child very well, takes responsibility for consideration of his welfare and development, and records in-depth observations of the child on a regular basis. I found this practice to have elements of both mainstream documentation and Waldorf child studies. At Lóczy, if an infant is experiencing difficulty in movement, the first consideration is the relationship with his primary nurse.

Similarly, within Lóczy's newly offered groups for parents with their infants and toddlers, great sensitivity is shown by the staff to the needs and feelings of the mothers. In the course, we were cautioned to employ common sense and careful consideration in our approach with parents, so that they would not be made to feel inadequate in any way. The goal, true to the Pikler model, is to safeguard the relationship between the parent and the child, for it is out of this tender and sacred relationship that healthy self-initiated movement can emerge.

Caregiving activities of feeding, dressing and bathing are viewed as opportunities for building this relationship. The infant is not viewed as an object to be acted upon—to be fed, for example. Rather, the infant is seen as a capable human being and is invited to participate at his own level in the feeding, which is viewed as a cooperative activity. The adult's responsibility is to make the child feel welcome, to read his cues and to take into account his individual preferences; for example, does this child prefer the cereal lumpy or smooth? The consideration of the child's preferences and the focus on self-initiated activity are similar to occupational therapist Jean Ayres' principle of activating the child's "inner drive" during sensory integration therapy.

The children at Lóczy become exceedingly capable in their self-care at an early age. However, the goal of the nurse is not to promote independence, but rather to share in the joy of the child's developing self-mastery. The nurse does not praise the child, but if the child looks at the nurse, then she will warmly acknowledge that she sees the child's accomplishment, or struggle. As a result of the intimacy experienced during the caregiving encounter, the child is "filled up," so that when he is placed in the playpen, he is happy to be on his own to move and play.

Pikler tried out these practices initially with her own first-born, and then used and developed them further in her private practice as a pediatrician over a ten-year period. Finally, Pikler employed them on a larger scale when she started Lóczy, directing the orphanage for 39 years.

A different rate of motor development at Lóczy

In the U.S., the vast majority of infants do not achieve verticality through their own efforts; they do not negotiate the gross motor sequence that leads to sitting or standing through self-initiated movement. Children are routinely put into positions they cannot achieve through their own efforts. This is the usual mainstream cultural practice from which our expectations for quality and timing of motor development arise, and is also the model pediatric therapists study in school.

Lóczy is the only place in the world I know of where gross, fine and oral motor development have been studied through the lens of unhurried, self-initiated motor exploration. The unhurried pace was beautifully expressed by Anna Tardos, current director of the Pikler Institute: "What's the rush? We have our whole lives to be vertical!"

For more than sixty years, caregivers at Lóczy have made detailed observations, taken photographs, made videos and conducted scientific studies. I will quote one study which I found particularly fascinating. In this study, which involved 591 normal infants with birth weights over 5.5 pounds, it was observed that the infants, on average:

> [T]urned onto the side at 17 weeks, onto the belly at 24 weeks, and from belly-to-back-to-belly at 29 weeks. They began creeping on the belly at 39 weeks, and then crawled on hands and knees at 44 weeks. They sat [sitting is defined as sitting simultaneously on both sitz bones with hands free] and stood up in the same week at 49 weeks. At 66 weeks (15 months), they took the first steps. At 72 weeks (17 months), they walked with ease.

These data have been averaged, so there is a substantial deviation surrounding each value, and the deviation becomes more pronounced as development proceeds.

In other words, in the Lóczy model, there are tremendous differences between the children, and motor milestones are reached significantly later than we would expect from our experience in the U.S. For example, many of us in the U.S. would worry and try to teach our child if he did not take his first steps until 15 months, the average age at Lóczy. Many of us would be proud if our child walked at an earlier age, thinking that he may be more advanced than other children. However, it may be that the timing is more a function of environment.

Faster development is not necessarily better. Activity that takes place in the horizontal plane, before verticality is achieved, lays an incredibly important foundation for later life. Some of the work of the remedial therapist is essentially a recapitulation of what an infant would do unassisted if placed on the floor to explore the wonders and possibilities for movement of his own body, and his relationship to the outer world. Why not give infants time and space to do their work? They know far better than we do as therapists and parents what they need!

An astute observation made by Emmi Pikler illustrates this point beautifully. In this model of self-initiated motor exploration, Pikler observed that infants whose parents had previous histories of back pain spent longer in the horizontal activities of rolling, belly creeping, and crawling on hands and knees before coming into the vertical positions of sitting and standing than did infants whose parents did not have histories of back pain. The infants who were genetically predisposed to back pain and who stayed in the horizontal longer, had more variety in their movements in the horizontal positions than did the infants who became vertical faster. Movement in the horizontal plane provides opportunities to strengthen and elongate the muscles and ligaments of the spine—opportunities not possible in the vertical position. It was as if the infants were working to prevent future back pain! Clearly, Pikler recognized the genius of the infant in his very individualized work on the floor, and she sought to create an environment whereby the infant would be free and unhindered to do this work.

Quality of movement

I was in awe of the grace, beauty, and efficiency of the infants' and toddlers' movements at Lóczy. Their balance, coordination and posture were extraordinary. Their movement possibilities were vast; they were very active and well-acquainted with transitional movements—that is, they did not remain in a few static positions, but instead moved in and out of positions easily. I did not see nearly the degree of drooling, low-tone trunks, wide-sprawling bases of support, compensatory high shoulders and stiffness, and other movement problems that I so often see in normal children in the U.S.

Integration of primitive reflexes

Among the children at Lóczy I also did not see abnormal retention of the primitive reflexes. Primitive reflexes are the involuntary stereotyped movements that are present in infants to help them survive in the early stages of life. By six to twelve months the primitive reflexes should become integrated, or fade away into the background of the child's movement repertoire. If they continue to manifest in the child's movements and aren't properly integrated, they are said to be abnormally retained and can negatively affect gross and fine motor coordination, sensory perception, behavior, and learning. It is very important for overall development that the primitive reflexes are integrated at the appropriate time.

When I inquired further of the staff about the lack of abnormal primitive reflex retention among the children at Lóczy, I was told that this is not an issue for them. Not an issue! There are pediatric therapists throughout the world who make a living treating children with abnormally retained reflexes. For twenty-eight years, I have witnessed increasing problems with proper integration of the primitive reflexes in normal American children with no history of prematurity or birth trauma. Children in the orphanage at Lóczy come from situations in which they were abused, abandoned or neglected—yet they are developing beautifully.

The nurses handle the infants in a way that promotes the integration of the primitive reflexes. The nurses' hands are extraordinarily sensitive to the muscle tone of the infant. They routinely wait for subtle tone changes to occur before the child is picked up and moved, and therefore the startle reflex is not set off and perpetuated. The infant is told what will happen before he is moved. The infant is bathed in the beautiful Hungarian language, which sounded almost like music to me, it was so soothing and calming. The infant's body is not forcibly moved; for example, a stiff arm is not shoved through a sleeve, but rather the sleeve is moved around the arm. The child is given intermittent eye contact, not so much as to make him nervous, but just enough to help him feel secure. The nurses do not rush or multi-task during the caregiving, and time seems to stand still. All these practices help to ensure that the child's central nervous system is not continually put into a "fight-or-flight" state. This more relaxed neurological state is conducive to promoting the process of reflex integration.

Development of balance as part of the gross motor sequence

The developmental progression of gross motor movements involves much more than is generally recognized and understood. For example, it includes lying on the back and looking at the hands; rolling from the back to the side and learning to lift the head and play with a toy in this position; rolling from the back to the stomach, to the right and to the left, and then across the room in order to get a toy; belly creeping; crawling and all of the steps up to walking, jumping, skipping and beyond. Throughout this complex and individualized gross motor sequence, the development of balance goes hand-in-hand with the integration of primitive reflexes. At Lóczy, opportunities for the infant to balance are countless! The infant is moved slowly by the nurse, and care is taken so that the infant can keep his balance while he is being moved.

In the infant, balance develops in two ways. It develops within each position primarily through subtle weight shifts. For example, the infant learns to reach for a toy while on his side without losing his balance and falling out of the position, and the infant learns to reach for one foot while lying on his back without losing his balance and falling over to the side. Balance also develops during the dynamic transitions between positions. We cannot develop balance for the child. The child has to do it himself and, therefore, must be actively engaged in order to lay down new neural pathways in the brain. If a child is put into a position that is too advanced for him, he won't be able to easily move within the position or into and out of the position. What matters is not how fast a child can arrive at, or is hurried to achieve, a developmental milestone. Rather, it's the child's quality of movement as measured by the sophistication of balance reactions within and between milestones that matters most.

At Lóczy, the children do what they are capable of doing. They are not expected to do what is yet too difficult for them. As a result, the infants do not strain while moving, but rather their movements are extraordinarily fluid, and enjoyable, and they move a lot. As I watched the infants at Lóczy, I wondered if they had a better than average chance of avoiding obesity and "the couch potato syndrome" later in life.

At Lóczy, infants are not propped up in sitting positions, they are not stood with their hands held and encouraged to walk, and baby equipment is not used. Instead, the infants are given tremendous time and space to execute self-initiated movements. Infants are even "allowed" to move during caregiving activities. For example, the changing table is larger than standard changing tables and has a railing around it so the child can move onto his hands and knees or can kneel or stand during a diaper change if he chooses.

When the infant pushes down against the floor, he comes up against gravity, and is learning to orient himself in relation to the supporting surface. This is a crucial component of balance. Another practice at Lóczy that supports the development of balance is that the infants are placed on a firm surface rather than a softer one. The firm surface increases proprioceptive feedback (that is, information from the muscles and joints that helps the child to understand unconsciously his body position in space), while a softer surface decreases proprioceptive feedback. So many of the children that I see with "gravitational insecurity," as it is known in sensory integration—that is, an exaggerated fear of and emotional response to movements that require losing contact with the ground, such as swinging and climbing—do not have this basic skill of knowing how to push down to orient themselves. Developing this inner sense of gravity's reliability through experiential interaction with one's outer surroundings is a key concept within Spacial Dynamics.

Development of focused attention

The children at Lóczy are very active, although not in a hyperactive way. In fact, I did not observe symptoms of ADHD or sensory processing disorders in the infants and toddlers at the orphanage. Instead, I observed a remarkable degree of focused attention in the children. I did not expect this, considering the children's histories—for example, some of the children were born to mothers with drug addictions. I did not observe the children being "entertained" or taught abstract concepts. Instead, they were exploring their world with joy and interest.

When I inquired about this remarkable degree of focused attention, I was told that the children are modulating their attention levels through unrestricted self-initiated movement. This concept is in alignment with basic principles of sensory integration, but I have never seen it carried out with such understanding. Therapists are not needed to prescribe sensory diets of specially designed, scheduled activities meant to provide adequate sensory input for the nervous system to become more self-regulated. Rather, the infants create and carry out their own sensory diets in the moment. This is possible through the carefully sculpted play environments provided for the children and through the generous time allowed for unhindered motor exploration.

At Lóczy, the development of attention has been observed and documented in depth. In approximately the first three years of life, periods of focused attention happen very frequently, although the periods themselves are short. The child will quiet his body and play with a toy for up to two minutes, and then he will need to move! The focused attention during fine motor exploration and the active large motor movements reinforce each other, and are necessary for one another. Perhaps the avalanche of ADHD diagnoses in the U.S. today is due in part to children simply responding to a profound lack of possibility for freedom of movement from infancy onward.

Crawling

I also asked about the frequency of crawling in the children at Lóczy. I learned that normal infants who have been at Lóczy from early infancy do not always roll or creep on their bellies, but they always crawl on hands and knees! I explained that in the U.S. many children skip crawling and use a hitching pattern instead, in which they sit upright with both legs to the side and, by pulling with one arm and pushing with the legs, slide their buttocks across the floor. Anna Tardos replied that once they had two or three children use the hitching pattern exclusively. After trying to understand why, they realized that the floor was too slippery! Three coats of lacquer had recently been applied to the wooden floor, and the infants' hitching made sense in relationship to their environment. (Since then, the floors get only one coat of lacquer.)

I was impressed that the staff held true to their belief in the inherent capacity of the infant to direct his own motor development, and that they did not intervene with hands-on therapy or try in any way to teach these children to crawl. Instead, they collectively questioned, observed, and reflected until, over time, the solution became clear.

A normal infant will self-initiate crawling if the environment supports this. There must be sufficient space and reason to crawl, e.g., in order to get something. If the toys are all within reach in a small space, there is no reason to crawl. Another interesting consideration is the type of footwear worn by the infant. If we had on skis, we would probably stand up in order to get somewhere rather than crawl. Similarly, if the infant wears a hard-soled shoe and is in a crib, this will promote pulling to stand rather than crawling. Another factor which decreases the incidence of crawling is simply that the child is not given ample time on the floor.

Applications for children with special needs

At Lóczy, it is believed that every child—including children with disturbances in their neuromotor and musculoskeletal systems—has the inherent capacity to guide his own motor development through self-initiated movement. Children with special needs receive traditional orthopedic care such as surgery and massage, but unlike the usual therapy in the U.S., they are not taught to perform a motor skill that they are not capable of performing on their own. Instead, infants with special needs are cared for with the same practices used for typically developing children, only perhaps in a more detailed manner. I observed carefully the children with special needs, and my sense was that they were slower in reaching the motor milestones compared to similar children in this country; however, in my evaluation the quality of their movements was superior, and they were much more actively engaged. Interestingly, these are the same observations I had for the normal children at Lóczy.

I observed one particular child with a quite serious orthopedic congenital defect, in that he was born without femurs, or thigh bones. At birth, the doctors had said that it was not possible for him to learn to walk. This child had been at Lóczy since early infancy, and had received loving, attentive care and the usual opportunities for self-initiated movement. When I observed this child in the orphanage, I was amazed to see him strolling around the block, walking up and down small hills, riding a scooter, and even trying to jump!

Pikler and Steiner

The principles employed at Lóczy are in alignment with Rudolf Steiner's recommendations that our goal is not to "fix" children, but rather to remove hindrances to their development. Steiner also advocated that the infant be allowed to come into the vertical on his own, working against forces of resistance in an archetypal battle to overcome gravity, thereby strengthening his will and coming into relationship to the three planes of space. This is exactly what Emmi Pikler did, with tremendous depth of understanding and penetration of practical detail.

A glimpse of archetypal development

I felt a kinship with the Lóczy staff in our shared respect and love for the deep mystery of the infant's motor development. There was a palpable understanding that the self-initiated unfolding of motor development provides something essential to the process of becoming a human being. My visit to Lóczy opened my eyes to the majesty of what is possible. It revealed a glimpse into the inherent genius of the infant in guiding his own motor development. And perhaps even more astounding, it offered one possible means by which this could manifest. I came home from Budapest filled with hope for what can grow—relevant to our own situations in this country—out of these invaluable insights.

Jane Swain is the associate director of the early childhood training course, "The Child and Family in the First Three Years" at Sophia's Hearth Family Center in Keene, NH, where they are planning a new facility that will include teacher training, parent-child classes and a childcare center which will incorporate the ideas of Waldorf early childhood education and Emmi Pikler into its practices. Jane is a pediatric physical therapist and is the movement education teacher for the primary grades at Monadnock Waldorf School in Keene, NH.

The Wonder and Complexity of Motor Development in Infants

by Vanessa Mitchell Kohlhaas

The infant's incredible journey through the stages of motor development shows the complexity and wisdom of the growing human body. Each stage carefully lays the groundwork for the next skill to emerge, and the child explores and practices every new skill with the interest and precision of a scientist. Gradually she moves toward the upright positions—lifting her head, balancing on all fours, sitting, pulling herself to a standing position—until she takes her first step. Each new stage is equally important for the healthy development of the whole child. This article gives a series of pictures of how a parent or caregiver might approach the infant during caregiving and playtime in a way that supports healthy, natural development.

Pikler, Gerber, and Steiner on free movement in infancy

Dr. Emmi Pikler, the Hungarian pediatrician who in the 1940s founded the orphanage known as the Pikler Institute in Budapest, and Magda Gerber, a child development specialist who brought Pikler's work to the U.S. and founded RIE (Resources for Infant Educarers), have provided insights into the child's development of movement. Their shared emphasis on observing the child's abilities in the moment (what he *can* do now), versus focusing on prescriptive developmental schedules (what *should be* achieved), respects the complexity of motor development during infancy. Their recommendation to allow the child to develop motor skills naturally, without intervention, allows the child to explore herself and the world around her out of freedom and without pressure.

The observations and practices of Pikler and Gerber support Rudolf Steiner's insights about infants' motor development by recognizing that we do not need to teach a child to walk, because a deep wisdom is present that guides the process. According to Steiner, allowing free movement, without hindrance or hurrying, creates space for the spiritual world to optimally support the child's development. This is illustrated by Steiner in the following passage:

> In childhood, a dream world still seems to hover about us. We work on ourselves with a wisdom that is not in us, a wisdom that is more powerful and comprehensive than all the conscious wisdom we acquire later. This higher wisdom works from the spiritual world deep into the body; it enables us to form the brain out of the spirit. We can rightly say, then, that even the wisest person can learn from a child…In the first years of life, however, this higher wisdom functions like a "telephone connection"

to the spiritual beings in whose world we find ourselves between death and rebirth. Something from this world still flows into our aura during childhood. As individuals we are then directly subject to the guidance of the entire spiritual world to which we belong. When we are children—up to the moment of our earliest memory—the spiritual forces from this world flow into us, enabling us to develop our particular relationship to gravity.[1]

It is through this connection to the spiritual world that the child is able to learn so much in a relatively short amount of time. As parents and educators, we can observe the child and ourselves so that we do not inadvertently create obstacles to this profound work that is not only physical, but also spiritual.

Through movement, the child determines where her body is in space and in relationship to solid ground, which leads to a feeling of centeredness and uprightness. The infant, in an archetypal battle over her limbs, gradually learns to gain control of the limbs so that she can be the vehicle of the will. A child who, through free movement, learns to feel grounded, settled, organized, and coordinated can meet the world with confidence.

Adjusting to a new environment

The newborn infant seems to be in a semi-conscious state, absorbing the sense world through her whole body. Only gradually will she learn to differentiate herself from the world around her. The newborn spends much of her time asleep, adjusting to her new environment. No longer is she protected from the outside world within the warm and sustaining womb of her mother. She now takes an active role in the fulfillment of her own needs, including breathing and feeding. This is no easy task, but she has been preparing for it even before birth.

The most important role of the parent during this stage of the infant's development is to provide protection and warmth, so that the child can more readily adjust to physical life on her own. This idea of providing warmth and protecting the senses of young children is an important principle of Waldorf early childhood education. Within the RIE/Pikler approach, this idea of protection of the senses takes on a slightly different form, in that the child is protected from startling sensory experiences through the parent's or caregiver's sensitive words and gestures. The parent or caregiver is encouraged to prepare the infant for what is coming through simple, gentle descriptions and respectful actions. For example, when the infant cries out in hunger, the mother can acknowledge the child's communication by saying, "Yes, I hear you. You are hungry. It is time for you to eat." Then, before picking the child up, the mother can avoid surprising or over-stimulating the child by holding out her hands and saying, "I am going to pick you up now. Are you ready to eat?" In a calm and slow manner, the mother takes her time to lift up her baby. Once they are settled and feeding begins, and the mother or caregiver is encouraged to remain focused and present so that a real connection can take place.

---

[1] Rudolf Steiner, *The Spiritual Guidance of the Individual and Humanity* (Hudson, NY: Anthroposophic Press, 1991), p.9. Original German edition published 1911.

Room to move

While lying on her back on the floor, the infant begins to develop more control over her movements. Her legs and arms bend and move as if she is swimming in space. On her tummy, she can lift her head for a moment and turn it from side to side. Then, one day, she makes a great discovery—her hands. These become a favorite plaything. She fascinates herself by exploring her own body and then moves out beyond her fingertips. Now her head can turn, her arm can stretch out in the same direction, and she can pick up a cloth or small toy with her hand. There is so much around her to take in and explore!

In a desire to have their infant close by at all times, some parents carry a car seat from room to room in the house during the early stages of development. But being contained in a car seat restricts the infant's free movement, as it is difficult for the child to turn and stretch while sitting in a curved chair. Providing a safe place for the infant to lie freely on her back is a healthy alternative. If there are older siblings or pets, a playpen or gates can be used to ensure safety. Rather than seeing this as a restriction to separate the child, the playpen or gates can be viewed as a way for the child to move around freely and safely. It creates the added benefit of freeing the parent to complete household tasks at times while the infant does her own work of exploring. Then, when the infant needs care, the parent can be more fully available for the child. This healthy balance of time together and time apart benefits both the parent/caregiver and the child.

In her own time

Sometimes a parent wishes to aid development by moving her baby into a position that she cannot yet master, such as sitting propped up with pillows. But the unassisted development of movement follows a specific sequence of skills that requires the child to be fully active during each stage. When a child is put into a new position before she is naturally ready, she loses the freedom to control her own movements. The propped infant is unable to move herself back into the lying position. She remains uncomfortably frozen in this new position or simply slumps over. On her back, however, she can turn and lift her head, move her legs, and reach out with her arms. And when she is tired from this new activity, she can simply relax back into the lying position.

The infant progresses from lying on her back to slowly turning and rolling over onto her belly. This does not happen all at once, but through many practice opportunities. While lying on her back, the infant stretches and flexes her muscles this way and that. She lifts her leg and crosses it over to the other side. Then, one day, she turns herself all the way over. Her arm might become caught underneath her. She will return to lying on her back and have a little rest before trying again. When she is able to roll over, in her own time, she will have already developed the skills needed to lift her head, free her arm and move her limbs while lying in the prone position. She may sometimes lift her head and all four limbs at the same time as if she is flying like a bird.

Creating a safe space for free movement

Once the child is mobile, gates can section off part of a room so that the parent can feel confident that the infant will not get hurt while freely covering ground. The space can then grow and change with the child. A playpen that was adequate when the child was non-mobile is too small for the infant now, except for brief moments. Careful observation and taking into account the baby's point of view help the parent or caregiver to determine whether the child has adequate space in which to move and explore.

An infant is a unique individual who deserves respect. She is in the process of discovery during free play, and so her caregiver needn't unnecessarily interrupt her or feel that she has to be an active playmate. A play space safe enough for the adult to feel comfortable allowing the infant to play in, without always remaining right next to her, is ideal. This way the parent can be close by, but can still engage in adult tasks. There are also moments for the adult to passively participate during the child's free play. The caregiver can learn so much from the child through observation, a time during which the infant can play until she is satisfied, without too much interaction. Of course, the caregiver would intervene in the case of a safety concern or when it is time for a diaper change, feeding or bath. Uninterrupted play enables the infant to learn so much, such as how things work, problem-solving, cause and effect, and concentration—all naturally and, again, in her own time.

Once the child can roll over and play in the prone position, she begins to develop more control over the movements of her body. She can easily lift and maintain her head and chest off the ground. Her legs have extended and developed more muscle tone. She begins to creep with her torso on the ground, pulling herself along and using her legs the way a lizard moves in the desert. Now the child has the ability to move across a room using a wide range of movements. She can turn her head and look in the direction a sound came from. She can pick up a toy and play with it while lying on her stomach, or she can navigate along the floor, encountering new possibilities for exploration.

This is also the time that a child may learn to sit on her own. Lying on her stomach, she is able to first lean on one side with her torso still on the ground. Then, using one of her arms, she is able to lift herself into a half-sitting position. Finally, she is able to sit up without using either arm as a support. With a little more practice she can sit with her legs stretched out and her arms free to explore objects around her. When a child is given the time and space needed to learn to sit on her own, she is often more at ease with her posture.

Supporting natural development

The play space can expand and change further as the child learns to sit and crawl, allowing for free movement. This is often the time that parents will consider using walkers or jumpers, but such equipment takes away freedom of movement and may even obstruct development. Playtime on the floor to creep, roll and explore allows the child a wide variety of movements so that her motor skills can continue to develop naturally. Pikler addresses the use of artificial equipment and exercises with young children with these words:

The question is not how we can "teach" an infant to move well and correctly, using cleverly thought up, artificially constructed, complicated measures, using exercises and gymnastics. It is simply a matter of offering an infant the opportunity—or, more precisely, not to deprive him of this opportunity—to move according to his inherent ability.[2]

Some simple caregiving choices can be helpful in this regard. For instance, nonrestrictive clothing that is, nonetheless, not too loose-fitting allows the newly mobile child freedom. Non-skid socks allow the child, when creeping, to gain sensory feedback from the floor. Sleeping sacks used during nap in cold weather means that the child is able to kick and move without the risk of throwing off needed blankets. Dressing the child in natural fibers ensures that she is not distracted by uncomfortable touch sensations and can stay more aware of her body's reaction to movement.

A new relationship to gravity

The child moves from creeping on her torso to crawling on her hands and knees. This stage of development gives the infant a new relationship to the earth and gravity. No longer is her body being pulled toward the ground, but, rather, she is able to take control and raise herself up. Crawling provides important movement patterns that may have far-reaching effects on the child's visual and cognitive skills, as well as on her continued development of movement. Infants learn eye-hand coordination skills by watching their hands as they crawl across the floor. And, of course, crawling provides the child with a new level of freedom.

Playing outside is a wonderful opportunity for all children, especially children who are crawling on all fours. Nature offers many interesting play materials such as leaves, dirt, sticks and rocks and so, of course, close supervision is needed. It also abounds with grass, hills, and logs to climb over and around. Outside playtime provides children with an intimate connection to the seasons and offers a challenging place in which to practice creeping so that the quality of their movements continues to improve.

The day finally comes when the child stands by herself and takes her first step. In order to walk the child must first be able to support her own weight, balance on one foot, and shift her weight from one side to the other. This is no easy task, but she has been diligently, and joyfully, preparing for it for a long time, through all the previous stages of motor development.

Steiner expressed the importance of learning to walk in *The Spiritual Guidance of the Individual and Humanity*:

It is significant that we must work on ourselves to develop from beings that cannot walk into ones that walk upright. We achieve our vertical position, our position of equilibrium in space, by ourselves. In other words, we establish our own relationship to gravity.[3]

---

2   Sensory Awareness Foundation, *SAF Bulletin #14: Emmi Pikler 1902 – 1984* (Mill Valley, CA: Sensory Awareness Foundation, 1994), p.6.

3   Steiner, ibid., p.11.

Honoring the child's inborn motivation

By quietly honoring children's intrinsic motivation, we support their natural joy in moving. For example, when a child is completely involved in walking, the parent might simply observe with a quiet smile and an attitude of respect for the accomplishment. Loud, enthusiastic praise—such as clapping and exclaiming, "Good!! Look at you! You are walking!"—can backfire. The child might then look over, lose her balance and fall. By allowing intrinsic motivation to continue to grow and develop in the child, the parent is helping to lay the foundation for a lifelong joy in learning.

The way infants instinctively and naturally move is always the safest. However, even when a child is given space and time to develop motor skills naturally, she will still occasionally fall. When a child falls, she is learning on a physical level how to protect her head when she loses her balance. This is a skill she will need again and again throughout her development, as walking progresses to running and jumping. The experience of falling and getting back up also supports the child's emotional growth, showing her that she is capable of continuing with an activity even when there has been a challenge along the way. It is often the parent's instinct to catch a child who is just about to fall. But holding back from rescuing the child too soon, too often, gives her a chance to regain her balance and continue on her way.

Learning to fall, get up, and move on is, perhaps, the best preparation for life.

☙

Author's Note: I have gained so much from the work of Steiner, Pikler and Gerber as a teacher and, most recently, as a new mother. My husband and I welcomed our son, Leon, into the world in October, 2007. It is such a gift to observe his development with interest and pleasure, but no agenda. I can recall vividly the first time that he rolled from his back to his stomach. He had been working at rolling over for weeks, sometimes with great frustration. But my husband and I trusted his ability and continued to give him time and space to make new discoveries. Then, one day, he finally rolled over. I was amazed that he was able to get his arm out from under his chest pretty quickly. He turned his head to me and smiled.

Of course, there are other moments that don't end in smiles. With each new accomplishment, Leon struggles and pushes himself to learn more. And I struggle as a mother right alongside him. I don't always parent the "Waldorf," "Pikler," or "RIE" way, but I am supported by the wisdom that I have been given. In the end, I remind myself that I will develop as a mother in my own way and in my time—in the same way that I strive to respect the young child's development. Anna Tardos, the current director of the Pikler Institute, provided me with this sage advice just before Leon's birth: "Do not think of what you have learnt and how to be a right mother. You only have to pay attention to the baby and do what comes from the heart."

Vanessa Kohlhaas currently leads the parent-child program at the Whidbey Island Waldorf School, north of Seattle, Washington. She completed her BA in Music at the University of Texas at Austin and went on to earn her special education teacher certification and work in a public preschool program for children with disabilities. She completed the Waldorf Teacher Training at Antioch University New England, receiving a master's degree. In addition to teaching parent-child classes, she has taught nursery and kindergarten in Waldorf schools. Vanessa and her husband Mark recently welcomed the birth of their first child, Leon.

Fostering Healthy Language Development in Young Children: A Journey in Relationships

by Susan Weber

The development of speech and language in the young child is truly a marvel, full of wonder for those who accompany its unfolding. We know intuitively that speaking arises from a mysterious place, one that has fascinated linguists for a long, long time. The Gospel of St. John begins with the very image of language development: "In the beginning was the Word." The creative energy of the Word is understood, in Rudolf Steiner's description, as a formative power, building even our physical bodies. It is no wonder, then, that coming into language is of such monumental importance, and that the adults in the young child's environment have such a profound influence on this process. The Word is a powerful force. Poets, writers, orators, and each of us change the world through our speech. Language is the gift the gods give to humanity for our creative activity.

This creative force of the Word can be experienced in the child's earliest expeditions into language. The child's magical made-up words, concrete descriptions of the world around him, and unique phrasings wake up our own hearing. The Word is fully animate to the child and each word contains a world within it: "I thought 'boxing' was a word that hit," a young child said to his mother. Backhoe becomes "hackbow," butterfly becomes "flutterfly."

At each stage of the first seven years of development, children delight us first with babbling, then with the utterance of "Mama" or "Papa," followed by words, names, phrases and increasingly complex syntax enriched by an ever-broadening vocabulary. Daily experience brings every detail of the child's environment into words. Many steps unfold as the child's language capacity grows. Eventually, our kindergarteners greet us with their rhyming word play, their interest in riddles they scarcely yet understand, and their extraordinary memory for each linguistic turn of phrase in a complex fairy tale.

But what comes in between? Most importantly, what is it that draws forth the child's ability to work, play, and live as a speaking human being? As with other capacities that unfold during the first three years of life, speech requires not only human relationship and example, but also the existence of forces within and beyond the child herself. Initially, the adult leads the child into speech and language through intimate relationship. Within this sacred space, the adult both speaks and listens, enabling the first communication through spoken language to come forth.

Clearly, for language to emerge there must be an "I" and a "Thou," adult and child. Over days and months, a foundation of nonverbal communication is built: a listening to one another without a single word. Is my baby hungry, or tired, or cold? Is mama coming to get me now? Is she happy to hear me? Will she feed me? The parent learns early to differentiate the language of crying, and also to observe and read the gesture of her child: Is she still hungry for another mouthful or has she turned her head away from the spoon, signaling that she is full, satisfied? Does she wish to be picked up from her crib? The baby stretches out her arms in a gesture of active openness, a gesture that tells a whole story. The child, too, learns to read the gestural as well as verbal communication of parents and caregivers.

The more sensitive and rich these elements of interpersonal communication are, the more deeply does the child become a communicating being. The adult welcomes the child by creating a spiritual space into which the child enters and dialogue arises. When the adult speaks with interest, warmth and respect, the child listens with her whole being. Without question, the adult's speech *toward* the child is central to this phase.

Gradually, the child's speech unfolds: he takes hold of his world and, as Karl König describes so artistically, words "rain down" upon him. Dialogue between adult and child about daily life, their mutual interests and activities, remains central. Tenderly the child begins to speak. But at first it is as if this capacity to express words is a secret between parent and child. Parents often say, "But he speaks so much at home!" And truly, the child's home—that protected space that is the child's world—is the mystery center in which the miracle of language blossoms. Step by step, the child will gradually select other adults with whom to speak—a grandparent, a neighbor, a playgroup leader, a friend's parent.

If we observe closely, we will see that young two-year-olds do not often converse with one another. One child will speak to the other, but the second child is seemingly deaf to the words, as if the child were not speaking to *him*. As adults, we still remain the primary language partners *and models*. Seen from the context of Rudolf Steiner's description of the twelve senses, our *sense of the word* has developed through the presence of our Ego. This enables the possibility for real listening, whereas before the child says "I" to himself at around age three this sense is not yet adequately active to enable true listening to the other.

But let us peek in at a group of four- and five-year-olds. As a community of speakers, they almost seem to exclude the adults. They now have a secret language among themselves! As the adults, *we* have receded into the background.

Language acquisition is a gradual process, individual for every child, with its numerous delicate transitions unfolding either quickly or slowly. The path is wholly individual, not unlike walking. Tremendously subtle linguistic structures have been built, and linkages have been created within the brain, the speech motor mechanism, and with the outside world. Invisible word-threads have been woven with the whole surrounding world, creating a tapestry that belongs solely to the child himself. We recall the stages:

- Babbling—The baby's earliest babbling encompasses all the sounds of the universe and all the language groups of the earth;

- Selection—The baby gradually selects out the phonemes of his own language, and sounds that he does not hear in his environment fall away;

- Encapsulation of meaning in words, then phrases, then "telescopic" phrases of noun and verb that express a complete concept.

All of these stages occur within the context of adults speaking to children. When does this most naturally occur during infancy? During those moments that arise out of personal relationship. And where is this relationship most logically and naturally expressed? It is within the activities of daily care—diapering, feeding, dressing, bathing. Emmi Pikler, through her work as a family pediatrician and later at the Pikler Institute in Budapest, recognized this aspect of the child's life as primary for the activation of many developmental themes for infants and toddlers. Magda Gerber also brought these insights from her experiences with Dr. Pikler to North America through her work in the United States at RIE (Resources for Infant Educarers).

Can any of us picture carrying out these basic caregiving tasks in silence? It is not easily imaginable. Observe mothers with their infants and young children. If we hear and observe silence, our pedagogical intuition is alerted, actively searching for a source, a reason, a path to understanding the genesis of this *unnatural* behavior.

The adult continuously expands the child's language through natural dialogue, embellishing and extending the conversation as the child's language becomes ever more expressive.

Those who have studied the work of the Pikler Institute and RIE cannot help but encounter in themselves a deep interest in the unfolding of language. The work of RIE often brings questions from Waldorf early childhood teachers about "talking to children," since we have been encouraged to work with the young child out of imitation, artistically and through gesture, to guide the child through his will and engagement with life. With children from three to seven, we can understand this way of working. However, with the child who is just coming into language or has not even begun to speak, something different is needed. The child's language organism awakens through stimulation from without, and we are the source of that stimulation.

Rainer Patzlaff's booklet, *Childhood Falls Silent*, originally published by the Australian Association for Rudolf Steiner Early Childhood Education, offers a compelling description of the situation for many children. In this booklet (now out of print, but soon to be available in an online version from AWSNA), Patzlaff cites research in which the physical imitation of the motor mechanism of speech from one human being to another was observed:

With great surprise kinesthetics found that the listener answers the perceived speech with just the same fine motor movements as the speaker unconsciously performs, also incorporating the whole body and with a delay of only 40 to 50 milliseconds, precluding the possibility of conscious reaction. Condon, the one responsible for this discovery, describes the astonishing synchronicity of movements in the speaker and listener as follows: "Figuratively speaking it is as if the whole body of the listener was dancing in precise and flowing accompaniment to the perceived speech." …It is as if both speaker and listener are moving in a common medium of rhythmic movement. And this applies only for speech sounds, not for noise or disjointed vowels, as repeated tests have proven…A two-day-old baby in the USA reacts to spoken Chinese with the same minute movements as to spoken American-English.[1]

At the Pikler Institute in Budapest, the caregiver develops her intimate relationship with each child not only through her touch and the sharing and playfulness that occur during caregiving times together, but also through her voice. In a musical, natural way, the caregiver engages the child with rich, rhythmic language; she speaks to the preverbal child from earliest infancy, and he responds with his eyes, his gestures of collaboration, his interaction. This is precisely the activity Patzlaff describes as essential for human development. "Whether we recognize it or not, we have an effect on the physical body of the child through the spoken word and we consequently influence the emotional and spiritual possibilities for the child's development later in life. Which of us is aware of this immense responsibility when we talk to a child?"[2]

How *do* we support the unfolding of language? This is a critically important question in our times in which children experience so much "mechanical" language, but less and less human discourse. Patzlaff details the decline in language capacity of children over the past several decades:

Joachim Kutsche found some bitter words for it [speech falling silent] in the magazine Der Spiegel *(38/1993): "Whether at home at the dinner table or in the car on the road, in German families (what's left of them), people don't converse. At most functional instructions are still in use: "Don't be so late!"; "Leave that!"; "Hurry up!"; and the binary answers of the little ones: 'Yes.' 'No.' 'Yes'…end of conversation.*

…In 1997 a leading insurance company felt compelled to publish a book with the title Talk To Me! *with the sole purpose being to stimulate parents to speak with their child!*[3]

The advent of the ubiquitous cellular telephone, hand-held movies, and recorded stories for little children in the course of the fifteen years since this research was shared only increases the urgency of our need to engage with our children through language. Clearly, children learn to speak by being spoken to. The musicality of the adult's speech with the infant bathes the child in the Word, introducing the holy capacity that makes us human. In the earliest stages of language development, it is essential that the adult speaks to the child. We are the *source* of language!

---

1   Rainer Patzlaff, *Childhood Falls Silent: The loss of speech and how we need to foster speech in the age of media* (Australian Association for Rudolf Steiner Early Childhood Education, undated) p.8. Originally published in German by the International Association of Waldorf Kindergartens, Stuttgart.

2   Ibid., p. 10.

3   Ibid., pp. 2-3.

We serve forever as models for children's language development, but in the later years of early childhood our role is transformed. As kindergarten teachers especially, the *functional* aspects of speaking recede and the *artistic* aspects—storytelling, poetry, recitation—come forward more strongly. The children speak with each other! Our stepping back creates the opportunity for *listening to* the child, for ensuring that he feels seen and heard as the individual he is becoming.

Our task as educators and caregivers is to understand and differentiate the kinds of speech that we offer to children in relation to their developmental stages. Language is an essential tool for providing the child with orientation in time and space, and in the early years, language together with gesture is intrinsic to guiding children.

One can picture a caregiver approaching a young child with the intention to pick him up for a diaper change. The adult's thoughts are clear, her intentions far along the path into will activity. But the child may be unaware of the adult's intention, and when the adult arrives, the child is only then entering into the process of participating in this caregiving activity. For the child to engage himself fully and comfortably in relaxed and happy anticipation, he needs time to prepare himself. He must change his focus, let go of involvement with his play or another activity, and recognize both the adult and the anticipated diapering. No matter how intimate the relationship, if the adult unexpectedly picks up the child without making eye contact and verbal contact, the child's startle reflex may be activated and he may express distress or, in a somewhat older child, resistance. Repeated activation of the startle reflex in this way may cause a child to sustain a high stress level, which over time interferes with healthy well-being in numerous ways. Alternately, when the adult approaches the child slowly and uses her voice to indicate her presence, when she orients the child through words and gesture about what will happen, the child now has a "response time." These precious seconds—the waiting, the respectful pause—make all the difference: "Hello, Sadie, I'm here for you. It's diaper time."

This simple, natural and direct approach is deeply integrated into the caregiving practices that have evolved at the Pikler Institute. Soft, melodic, musical speech accompanies all caregiving activity, serving to engage the child delicately, stimulate his own language development, and build the relationship between adult and child.

However, these conversations do not involve the kind of aimless chatter or premature conversations that draw a child out of his *doing* by bringing unneeded consciousness to his activity. But the older child who has unfolded a life of fantasy and imagination is a very different being from the infant or toddler just beginning to savor the joy of language, the power of speaking, and the intimacy of words exchanged with others.

With toddlers, the adult's language is also crucial to helping them navigate situations involving conflict with other children. Children need to know boundaries and to receive strategies for problem-solving from the adults around them. Once the period has passed in which distraction is effective as a strategy for guiding behavior, young children *want* and *need* to engage their peers and adults in conflict, to test their emerging feeling of self and to understand themselves in the context of social relationships. As adults, we help children navigate this transition through our loving support and our gift of language. We express boundaries for appropriate and inappropriate behavior through speech, and through our words we offer simple solutions for toddler conflict.

As adult speakers in the child's environment, we are the bridge that enables the child to unfold her full humanity. Rhythm, cadence and the metric forms of the mother tongue are offered throughout the child's waking hours as invitations to step further into living relationship with others. We pass to the child the gift of language once given to us. Through our activity as human beings who speak with one another, the holy journey begins.

☙

Susan Weber has been a public school teacher and administrator, Waldorf early childhood teacher, and Waldorf early childhood teacher training coordinator at Antioch University New England, where she also previously earned a certificate in Waldorf early childhood education. She was among the founding circle of Sophia's Hearth Family Center in Keene, NH, and is presently the Center's director. Sophia's Hearth Family Center provides community-based programs for parents, infants and very young children as well as training for professionals. The work arises out of the insights of Waldorf early childhood education, and is enriched by the work of the Pikler Institute.

Susan has completed RIE Level I training in Los Angeles, and introductory and advanced training at the Pikler Institute in Budapest, Hungary. She presented the work of Waldorf education in developing parent-infant and parent-toddler programs at the Pikler Institute's Sixtieth Anniversary Symposium in Budapest, Hungary, in April 2007.

Thinking and the Consciousness of the Young Child

by Renate Long-Breipohl

The first three years

Recently while observing young children in a child care situation, I watched one little boy around the age of two who was totally immersed in moving blocks into various positions. He stayed absorbed in his activity without looking up or saying a word. Does he think? Something *is* happening within this child that I want to understand in order to adjust the environment around him so that nothing disrupts his concentrated activity.

My own study of the subject of thinking set me on a journey: I re-read essential works on the first three years, looked at developmental research, and observed children whenever the opportunity arose. Here I would like to share some aspects of my work in progress that relate to coming to terms with thinking as an adult, the development of thinking as a process during the first three years, and events occurring in the third year of life.

To say it bluntly, thinking is not a favorite activity of our time. While we are surrounded by an endless variety of products based on sophisticated human thought and created by a fairly small group of highly trained engineers and designers, the actual process of thinking for oneself is experienced as stressful by many contemporaries. Students often find it strenuous to pursue a train of thought related to a question, and teachers find it difficult to engage students in processes that require concentrated thinking activity.

In adult learning, more and more visual aids are appearing, and the more they are used, the less we need to engage inwardly in a thinking process. This one can experience as an average computer user or by perusing a typical student textbook. It all comes down to information intake and information processing, following ready-made pathways or existing mental frameworks. Knowledge is broken up into small paragraphs, the main thoughts are boxed so that one can take them in at a glance and, overall, there is an abundance of accumulated information. Steiner predicted that human beings would gradually lose the ability to think, and yet he regarded the human faculty of thinking as the gateway to spiritual development.

What is the faculty of thinking in human beings?

It is important to have an understanding of what thinking is when we approach children. Thinking is an activity that takes place within the inner realm of the human being and, in its highest aspect, is wisdom in individualized form. One can describe thinking as a supersensible faculty, since it does not derive its essence from sense experience. Thinking cannot be perceived directly by others. Concepts are formed and woven together through the activity of thinking, and in everyday life these concepts assist us in ordering, structuring or giving meaning to experiences.[1]

Through thinking we are free to reach toward high spiritual ideals, but our thinking can also be reduced to rationalizing our wishes, desires and actions. Then it binds itself too deeply to the material aspect of existence and is in danger of hardening and losing its connection to truth. The destiny of thinking is a theme to which Steiner returned in his lectures again and again. In our time many people find it difficult to devote themselves to thinking as a spiritual activity, or to think freely. However, one needs to consider thinking as a spiritual activity if one wants to find the key to thinking in the young child, as I will further elaborate in this essay.

Child development and thinking

In his book *Spiritual Guidance of the Individual and Humanity*, Rudolf Steiner spoke about the first three years of life and the evolving human being.[2] He described how learning to walk, to speak and to think is a three-step process in which the growing, incarnating child adapts to earthly conditions, and in which essentially spiritual faculties take hold in the child under the guidance of higher spiritual beings. Through this process, faculties gained in the spiritual world are transformed and reappear as the human faculties of thinking, feeling, and willing. These faculties develop within the bodily processes of achieving an upright position, turning the speech organs into instruments for the expression of language, and molding the brain into an instrument for thinking. Finally, in the third year, an evolving ability to think connects the child to the world community of human beings.

Active within these processes is the "I," which through walking orients the body to three-dimensional space, and through speech attunes the child's soul to a specific human community according to the individual destiny of the child. This activity of the I can be described as the streaming in of spiritual forces from a spiritual aura around the child. It is a process of which the child has no conscious awareness.

From this picture of human development questions arise regarding thinking in the young child. Why is the development of thinking primarily identified as occurring in the third year of life? Is it not a continuous process? What is our understanding of recent neurodevelopmental research that interprets early responses of babies to stimulation as forms of intelligence and that points to the ability of very young children to communicate from day one? And if there were a major leap in the development of thinking in the third year, why, then, would one wait until the seventh year before addressing the child's thinking in education, as Steiner has suggested?

1   Michaela Glöckler, *Gehen, Sprechen, Denken* (Walking, Talking, Thinking; not translated) (Stuttgart: Internationale Vereinigung der Waldorfkindergärten, 1997), p. 40.

2   Steiner, Rudolf, *The Spiritual Guidance of the Individual and Humanity* (Hudson, NY: Anthroposophic Press, 1992), pp. 3-24.

The first and second years in relation to thinking

It is generally acknowledged that thinking develops in the young child in accordance with the maturation and differentiation of the brain and nerve-sense system. It is interesting that Steiner spoke about thinking as a spiritual, as well as an earthly, faculty; he said that thinking originates in pre-earthly existence as a supersensible faculty of the human being, yet it is also active in and bound to earthly life through sense experience.

There are two aspects to thinking in the young child: The first relates to the supersensible nature of thinking, which is linked to the etheric body. In the very young child these etheric forces are still active from outside, sculpting and fine-tuning the head and bodily organs, without the child being conscious of it. "Connecting threads develop in the brain, and the forces which organize the connecting threads are seen by the clairvoyant during the first few weeks of the child's life as something that is forming extra sheaths for the brain."[3] The etheric body is still engaged in shaping the brain and radiating into the rest of the body.[4] This image often appears in children's drawings in which rays are depicted around the head of a human figure, connecting it to the world beyond.

I remember an eight-month-old child in a restaurant, sitting in a high chair, enthralled with a spoon he held in his hand; he moved it from one hand to the other. He licked it, turned it upside down and moved it faster and faster until the spoon fell to the ground. Does thinking play a part in such an activity?

Georg Kühlewind[5] points out that a young child absorbed in exploration lives naturally in a state of pure attentiveness, which may be achieved in adults only after intense practice in awareness. He describes pure attentiveness as an advanced stage of thinking activity, based on the ability to maintain the intentional quality of the will without pouring it into action. He calls it "soft will," that is, will purely within the activity of thinking. The child is able to be in this state of attentiveness naturally and is fully devoted to the object of his exploration.

This attitude of surrender is also found in the ability of the young child to imitate, an ability present from the very first stages of life. Steiner points to how thinking is dependent on imitation: "The child learns to think because it is an imitative being, wholly given up to its environment. It imitates what happens in the environment under the impulses of thoughts."[6] Sense experience and thinking are one. The child imitates and simultaneously is able to understand what is going on the moment the sense perception happens.[7]

---

3   Rudolf Steiner, *Understanding Young Children: Excerpts from Lectures by Rudolf Steiner Compiled for the Use of Kindergarten Teachers* (Silver Spring, MD: Waldorf Kindergarten Association, 1994), p. 55.

4   Rudolf Steiner, "The Child Before the Seventh Year" in *Soul Economy and Waldorf Education* (Hudson, NY: Anthroposophic Press, 1986), p. 112.

5   Georg Kühlewind, "Learning from the Child to be Human." *Kindergarten Newsletter UK* (Issue 36, 1999), p. 5.

6   Rudolf Steiner, *Education and Modern Spiritual Life* (Blauvelt, NY: Steiner Books, 1989), p. 77.

7   Michaela Glöckler, "The Birth of the Etheric" in *A Deeper Understanding of the Waldorf Kindergarten* (Silver Spring, MD: Waldorf Kindergarten Association of North America, 1993), p. 45.

Steiner speaks about the work of the "I" in the first three years as molding the brain. Two important influences are part of this process: Sense activity on the one side, leaving imprints of sensations in specific areas of the brain (as described by Eugen Kolisko in *The Bodily Foundation of Thinking*), and movement on the other. Steiner uses the term "bodily geometry" for the movement of the young child that allows her to find her place within spatial dimensions. Thinking is prepared through both activities.[8] Thinking and movement, originating from head and limbs, form a polarity that organizes development during the early childhood years. The head pole relates to the etheric forces working from the head downward, and the limb pole relates to the human soul-spirit or "I" working from the lower part of the body upwards. This is the organizing principle that underlies the process of coming into uprightness during the first year of life. The "I" activity of movement has an influence on the healthy development of thinking. Steiner's spiritual research into this process is now confirmed by developmental research and the therapeutic practice of stimulating thinking through movement.

As the child approaches the end of the first year of life, we may assume that the processes of intensive looking, touching, moving, and exploring have left within him many imprints, mental images which, however vague they may be at first, will eventually be met by concepts formed through the inner activity of the child.

A new quality is added to those early internal pictures flooding through the child once the child can anchor them in speech. Now words become the vehicle for the development of thinking. "Just as speech develops from walking and grasping, in short from movement, so thought develops from speech…and since the child is one great sense organ and in his inner physical functions also copies the spiritual, our own thinking must be clear if right thinking is to develop in the child from the forces of speech."[9]

Karl König has beautifully summarized the process of speech acquisition in *The First Three Years of the Child*, in which he describes how the child progresses from expressing physical well-being or physical needs to expressing his relationship to the outer world in words (naming) and, increasingly, in short sentences. Speech mirrors the child's being in relationship to objects and people. It links the child to the fine nuances of feeling expressed in language. How does thinking manifest at this stage of development?

Recent developmental research has described how adults can stimulate memory in children between the ages of one- and two-and-a-half years if in the presence of the child adults verbally recollect recent events of the child's life.[10] Russian educational psychologist Lev Vygotsky (1896-1934) suggested that intellectual development depends on the adult's verbal communications being slightly above the child's current level of communication.[11] His observations are interesting in that they point

8   Rudolf Steiner, *The Child's Changing Consciousness* and Waldorf Education (Hudson, NY: Anthroposophic Press, 1988), p. 19.

9   Rudolf Steiner, *Education and Modern Spiritual Life*, p. 112.

10   Laura E. Berk, A *Study Guide for Child Development* (Massachusetts: Viacom, 1997), p. 277.

11   Vygotsky's ideas are outlined in Berk, pp. 247-250.

to the connection between speech and thinking. Could one say that the child, through the adult as model, is able to imitate memory activity?

Thinking in the child who is approaching age two can be observed in the child's solitary play. The child moves objects, covers them, puts them side-by-side or on top of each other. The purpose is solely to make contact with the world of objects and to change their positions. Steiner states that it is through this interplay with the environment that the child finds his way spontaneously into thinking. While observing a child engaged in such play, one can experience concentrated attention. If the child has sufficient opportunity to play without disturbances, this mood will be recreated in play for years to come.

Thinking in the third year of life

What is the gift of the third year of life? The soul-spiritual forces in the child now complete their work on the foundations of the child's faculty of thinking. The I of the child has penetrated the physical body, the limbs, the rhythmic system, and the head. At the same time some part of the etheric forces of the head are freed. "At the age of two and a half, the child's head organization is developed far enough for those forces of the ether body which have been working on it to become released...acting now as soul and spiritual forces [available for other developmental tasks]."[12]

What can be observed in the child of this age? A vivid memory, a more elaborate way of speaking, original word creations and thought connections. The child enjoys playing with words, turning them around, inventing new ones—and he can surprise us with his own original ways of arranging syntax or linking sense impressions. Speech develops in leaps and bounds. This stage of development shows new achievements of thinking in everyday life. It becomes easier to follow routines, because the child can understand more of the meaning of what is done. Therefore it becomes easier to guide the child. In talking with the child, she seems more able to take in what is said. It is fascinating to observe in children of this age that they not only are creative in inventing their own words, but also in producing their own logic. Interestingly, the very individual and unusual thought connections of a three-year-old do not arrive out of a conscious thought process, but seem to emerge often unexpectedly, as if from somewhere else.

It is tempting for the educator who witnesses these new faculties as they arise during the third year to approach the child's thinking capacity with formal instruction. The ability of the child to process instructions addressing the intellect at age two has been documented in developmental research and has been utilized in program development for early childhood education. The third year is when many early learning programs begin.

One can understand the motivation for using learning materials such as picture and word cards to support concept building, verbalization or memory, since the thinking potential is there in the child and can be called up. But the constant involvement of an adult is needed to keep this process going.

12   Steiner, *Soul Economy and Waldorf Education*, p. 117.

What is learned at this age is not retained unless it is continually repeated. Steiner has warned of the consequences of adult intervention and demands on thinking and memory before the age of three: "What then will happen, if we make too great a demand on the intellect, urging the child to think, into thinking as such? Certain organic forces that tend inwardly to harden the body are brought into play. These forces are responsible for the salty deposits in the body and for the formation of bone, cartilage and sinew—in all those parts of the body, in short, that have a tendency to become rigid. This normal rigidity is over-developed, if intellectual thinking is forced."[13] It is of great importance that those who live with young children understand the spiritual background of the capacity to think. Steiner affirmed that we are to become, and need to become, free-thinking beings in order to develop our humanness.

"When the child learns to think—well, in thinking we do not remain in the realm of the individual at all. In New Zealand, for example, people think in exactly the same way we do here today. It is the entire earth realm to which we adapt ourselves, when as children we develop thinking out of speech...In thinking, we enter the realm of humanity as a whole."[14] In each child this possibility is established and in that respect the third year can be regarded as a culmination point of early development, representing in seed form the essence of the human being. This needs to be acknowledged in everyday life, so that one does not merely familiarize the child with thought processes related only to the immediate material environment and mundane situations. Often adults take pride when the child can already express himself intellectually in a way similar to older children or even adults. Yet too much praise and encouragement of the child's intellect can cause the child's thinking to become fettered to fixed thought-forms and prevent the child's thinking from flowing creatively and freely between the two worlds of thought: the spiritual and the earthly.

Only the emergence of consciousness of self around or shortly after age three will bring the child's thinking closer to the earthly realm and change the sense of "It thinks" into "I think." This step indicates that the child has become more conscious of himself as different from others and from the surrounding world. He has to leave the experience of oneness behind; it is the price for becoming an individual. From this time on, the child will feel himself as the originator of his thoughts.

It is important to notice that I-consciousness is achieved only after the I has been active in the process of brain development and, thus, in establishing the possibility of thought as a universal human activity. Steiner has stated that even though the child might use the word "I" correctly already at around the age of two-and-a-half, the appearance of I-consciousness happens after the age of three. In developmental psychology, the same phenomenon is called "the emergence of the psychological self" at around age three.[15] Professor of child psychology Laura Berk, a researcher and author on child development, also describes phenomena of "metacognition" in the child, such as the use of the words "think," "remember," and "pretend," and the child's realization that thinking is going on inside his head.[16]

---

13 Steiner, *Education and Modern Spiritual Life*, p. 122.

14 Steiner, *The Child's Changing Consciousness* and Waldorf Education, p. 55.

15 Berk, p. 279.

16 Berk, p. 281.

There is a deep wisdom in the sequence of development as I have outlined above. Thinking is not a personal achievement in the first place, but is established within us under the guidance of higher beings. Thinking becomes personal through consciousness of self, but always encompasses the possibility of expanding beyond the individual into the universal realm of thought. Stimulating self consciousness at an early stage poses the danger of closing the door to the universally human realm.

However tender and immature this consciousness of self may be, there is a general eagerness in educators to use this emerging consciousness of the child for reflecting and reviewing processes, such as making choices and decisions. These may relate to the child's actions, social situations, daily routines, food and clothing. But consciousness of self is a double-edged sword. It requires maturity to handle it, more maturity than can be expected of a three-year-old. In becoming conscious of their wishes and choices, some three-year-olds are overwhelmed by their own desires and become demanding. They also may change their minds quickly and can appear swayed by emotions. In such cases, parents often complain about their child's self-centeredness. Some children, when made conscious of their actions, become overwhelmed and react with insecurity, lack of confidence in their abilities, and fear of failure. It happens as early as three years of age that children say, "I don't like my drawing," or "I can't do that." Steiner speaks about this early appearance of consciousness of the I as a great mystery and, in a certain sense, as being premature.

Some educational conclusions

Modern education has regarded and used the child's ability to think as an opportunity to introduce early instruction. Undoubtedly there will be more research identifying the potential of the child to think at an ever earlier age. Programs have been designed for stimulating aspects of the young child's thinking, such as memory, color and form discrimination, and concept building. With this the child's thinking becomes tuned to the particular mode of abstract intellectuality prevalent in our time.

Steiner recommended strongly that we to leave alone the child's capacity for thinking at this stage, avoiding outer intervention. He was not concerned about intellectual progress, but, rather, about morality. In 1906 he wrote, "[Young] children do not learn by instruction or admonition, but through imitation. The physical organs shape themselves through the influence of the physical environment. Good sight will be developed in children if their environment has the proper conditions of light and color, while in the brain and blood circulation the physical foundations will be laid for a healthy moral sense if children see moral actions in their environment. If before their seventh year children see only foolish actions in their surroundings, the brain will assume the forms that adapt it to foolishness in later life."[17] Steiner points to the link between thinking and morality, on which depends the future of humanity. He is concerned with how the quality of adult thought influences the child. Therefore he emphasizes the self-education of the adult. "The education during these first two-and-a-half years should be confined to the self-education of the adult in charge who should think, feel and act in a manner which, when perceived by the child, will cause no harm."[18] And again, "Why have so many people 'nerves' today? Simply because in childhood there was no clarity and precision of thought

17   Rudolf Steiner, *The Education of the Child in the Light of Anthroposophy* (Hudson, NY: Anthroposophic Press, 1996), p. 19.

18   Steiner, *Soul Economy and Waldorf Education*, p. 115.

around them during the time when they were learning to think after having learnt to speak…The organs and vessels develop after the models of love, truth and clarity."[19]

How might this understanding change our approach to young children in our care? We may find ourselves paying more attention to our own thinking and how that might relate to the child's thinking. There is already among Waldorf educators an awareness regarding the importance of self-education and self-development, as well as a recognition of how speech relates to thinking. But as yet not enough attention is paid to the detail of the child's play in the third year of life. As Waldorf early childhood educators, we should make ourselves heard in the general field of education, where the child's intellectual development is so heavily emphasized. If we are clear in our own understanding of the child's development of thinking, then other educators will be open to what we have to offer, and more children will therefore benefit from educational and childcare practices that truly support them.

Let us return to the example of the child playing at the beginning of this essay. This play expresses the child's activity of thinking before the emergence of a consciousness of the I. This play of the young child marks a specific stage in development and should not be seen merely as a precursor to the "real" play of four- and five-year-olds.

Sometimes one will find that among Waldorf early childhood educators there is too little differentiation in how they approach the play of the child under the age of three versus that of the child over three. Steiner describes the very young child at play as a "hermit," totally immersed in his own world. This play needs to be nurtured by providing a quiet space and adjusting the daily rhythm to allow for the unfolding of undisturbed individual play. Through this play, the child weaves his connection to universal human thought before being drawn into an awareness of himself.

Often the rhythm of the kindergarten day is used as a model for the rhythm of the day in play groups and childcare settings intended for younger children. But is it appropriate for children under three to be interrupted in play in order to make space for group activities such as the morning circle? What is the right daily structure for this age group? How can one create a balance between togetherness and the child's natural desire to follow his own inner impulse? One can find answers to these questions by observing young children and by becoming more and more attuned to the wonderful processes of thinking in the young child.

Bibliography

Glöckler, Michaela. *A Healing Education* (Fair Oaks, CA: Rudolf Steiner College Press, 2000).

König, Karl. *The First Three Years of the Child* (Edinburgh: Floris Books, 1998).

Kolisko, Eugen, MD. "The Bodily Foundation of Thinking" in *The Threefold Human Organism* (UK: Kolisko Archive Publications, 1977).

☙

19   Steiner, *Education and Modern Spiritual Life*, p. 112.

Renate Long-Breipohl holds a doctorate in theology and a degree in education, majoring in early childhood education. She has been involved in Anthroposophy for 30 years. Before migrating to Australia in 1985 she has lectured in early childhood at universities in Bochum and Dortmund in Germany. In Australia she became the co-founder of the Samford Valley Steiner School near Brisbane and taught there in the kindergarten for 10 years. In 1997 she moved to Sydney to join Parsifal College, as a tutor in the Anthroposophical Studies course and as coordinator and tutor in the early childhood courses. Renate regularly travels, lecturing in Australia and the South East Pacific Region. She has coordinated Steiner early childhood teacher training courses in Manila, Philippines from 2000-2002 and in Bangkok from 2003-2006. She is member on the board of the International Association for Steiner Early Childhood Education.

Caregiving as an Art

The Sacred Art of Observation

by Theresa Catlin

When teachers observe children, it is common practice to carry in mind the goal of understanding the needs of a particular child or the dynamics of a group of children. In the fall of 2007, the opportunity to serve as an intern in two RIE (Resources for Infant Educarers) programs gave me the chance to approach observation in a different way. At Pacific Oaks College in Pasadena, CA, from September to December 2007, I observed one class for infants and another for toddlers. For three hours every Saturday, I simply observed children without any goal in mind. I made an astounding discovery: there is another way to observe, a way that both reveals the child and draws forth my own intuition. I call it deep observation.

Deep observation takes us to the heart of being with a child. Something new unfolds within us. This kind of observation is not born of intellectual curiosity; it is not even the practice of observing while holding a question. Observing takes the place of any judgments, comparisons or evaluations.

My experience of deep observation developed through the course of my RIE training. RIE encourages the adult's sensitive observation during children's play—it is one of RIE's "Seven Principles." During my internship I developed the practice of sitting quietly and unobtrusively, allowing my breathing to become deep and even. As my mind began to relax, I let go of a sense of purpose and striving. Something profoundly new now had a chance to emerge: a gentle state of presence, a deep listening. A new way to perceive thus began to develop within me.

Deep observation can awaken us to a more authentic, whole, and in-tune relationship with the children in our care. We observe in a sacred way, a way that allows us to truly receive the child as he or she is in the moment. Sometimes there is a sense of seeing the "whole child," a gestalt experience of his or her essence. Sometimes one is drawn to a certain aspect of the child's movement, or of her body—the way she uses her toes to search her surroundings, or shifts her weight just so, how she picks up the ball or moves her head forward to accept the bib. When we are in this state of deep observation, we are not looking for results or solutions—although profound insights may indeed arise in the instant, with resounding clarity and wise authority. There may also be hidden gifts in the moment of observation, not yet apparent. Perhaps this deep looking plants a seed that will bear fruit at some later time. A stronger connection with intuition may result.

Dr. Gerald Karnow, keynote speaker at the February 2008 conference of the Waldorf Early Childhood Association of North America, has similarly noted that, in observing children, we must empty ourselves of preconceptions, goals and opinions. Drawing from the insights of Rudolf Steiner, Karnow said that the observer needs to develop a posture of creative not-knowing, which involves pure, open receptivity. When we are able to become empty, still, quiet and utterly warm toward the child we are observing, Karnow said, we can have an inspiration of what we need to do—an inspiration that is achieved through creative identification with the being of the other person. "I must be willing to say, 'I don't know,'" he said. "With pure observation, we hold back the dis-ease of not having a ready answer."

Eventually, life's activity brings us out of observing—back to words, engagement and interaction. We resurface again, in ordinary time, but we are not exactly the same. Perhaps an increased understanding has come to us in the absence of striving toward it, and we wonder how to work with this new insight. Immediate action may not necessarily be the right response. Sometimes patience and more watchful waiting are what are called for. We can trust that, in time, we will know, deeply and calmly, what to do, or not to do.

Deep observation can be a gift to the child or children in our care, to the parents in our parent-child classes, and to ourselves. How to do it? Breathe, be still, and simply observe the child before you without interpretation. Insight may be a reward, though not always. When we allow the art of observation to remove expectations, we might just come upon a deeper sense of wonder, of rekindled joy, as we simply behold the child before us.

Theresa Catlin, the mother of two grown daughters, has been a Waldorf class teacher for eight years. She is a graduate of the LifeWays and Sophia's Hearth trainings on caring for young children, and is currently becoming a RIE affiliate. She leads parent-child and parenting classes at Highland Hall Waldorf School in Northridge, CA, and at her home studio.

In Their Shoes:
Reflections on Cooperative Caregiving

by Kristin Fiegl

On my final morning of the training course at Sophia's Hearth Family Center in Keene, New Hampshire, this past summer, I paused in my flurry of activity to take a moment for breakfast. I had just sprinted from the campground's showers to the little cabin our family had occupied during a week of rain showers, and was greeted by a floor strewn with air mattresses, rain boots and crates of food. Even though my body had come to rest, my mind was still racing: I found myself thinking back to yesterday's discussion on the care of young children, wondering how to best go about packing, and checking my watch to be sure that I wasn't running late. Then, my eyes came to rest for a moment on my children. My then four-year-old son was sitting next to his fourteen-month-old sister, who was lying on her back, just emerging from sleep. "Your sock fell off," he said. "Do you want me to help you put it back on?" In answer, she stretched her foot out to him. I breathed out, watching with her as he gently put on her sock.

It was an exchange that I easily could have missed. But a series of experiential exercises brought by Ute Strub of the Emmi Pikler Haus (a residential home for children in Berlin, Germany) over the final week of the training at Sophia's Hearth made it particularly significant. The exercises—which draw from the insights of Emmi Pikler about how to bring presence and respect to the care of young children, and which also reflect Rudolf Steiner's understanding of the spiritual nature of early childhood—considerably deepened our understanding of the young child. Almost without exception, the exercises were powerful experiences; finding the words to articulate the depth of learning and awareness that accompanied them is nearly impossible, and doing so almost conflicts with their nature. Also, as a group, we found that our individual reactions to the exercises varied greatly, and sometimes were completely opposite. And to write about these exercises is to risk taking something away from a reader who hasn't yet experienced them. So, for these reasons, and because I don't want to give away Ute's secrets, I will focus specifically on two exercises that served to highlight the value of cooperative caregiving.

The first student exercise was meant to simulate dressing a child. We each paired up and took turns putting on and taking off a buttoned shirt over our partner's clothes. Simple enough, it seems. We had all marveled at the level of caregiving we had witnessed in videos of nurses at the Pikler Institute dressing babies and toddlers. The children and their caregivers worked together as dance partners, seeming to anticipate each others' moves, pausing to let the other catch up, moving comfortably in a familiar routine. While most of us might never achieve the level of care provided by these caregivers, our group understood that it was important to approach dressing a child with sensitivity and respect.

Easier said than done. When it was my turn to take the role of the caregiver, I enjoyed making a connection with my partner, but still had the nagging feeling that I was fumbling. Dressing another person felt awkward—even though this was someone I knew! It reminded me of just how intimate the act of dressing is. I also found it difficult to know how much to speak to my partner. I wanted to give her a sense of what was to come by giving her some direction: "Now I'm going to pick up your arm…Now I'm going to put your arm in your sleeve…Here comes your hand." But as the exercise went on, I began to feel like I was babbling. When I help my own two children dress, I don't talk to them nearly as much as I did during the exercise. A large part of our "dance" is subtle, involving gesture and anticipation of the other's movements, in patterns that have been learned over time. But with my student partner, I was unsure how much assistance she wanted, or how much she wanted to dress independently. In another setting, we might have discussed that, but she was instructed to act as if she were a very young child. While my talking was meant to reassure her, and maybe it did to some degree, I was also talking to make myself more comfortable and to keep myself focused. (Ute shared later that while it's important to speak with the child during these caregiving moments, one can also speak "internally" as a way of staying present—this can help us avoid too much talking, yet also keep our thoughts from wandering.) While we were given plenty of time to complete the exercise, in my discomfort I hurried the process along, and felt some relief when it was over.

To be on the other side, playing the role of the young child, was altogether different. I had some initial discomfort before the exercise, but once my partner directed her attention toward me, I was soon calmed by her gentle and focused presence. She may have felt uncertain during the process—many of us did to some degree when we were the caregivers—but, as the receiver of care, I did not sense uncertainty. Ute asked us to share immediately what we felt after each of the exercises, before we had time to reflect on our own and others' experiences. With this exercise, I remember feeling the attention of my caregiver, focused solely on me and the task at hand. I also felt a sense of timelessness, of fullness in the space and in the unhurried pace of the experience. A few moments of this left me feeling nourished and "full"—a feeling that stayed with me a good while after the exercise finished. I don't remember now how much my partner helped me, how much she talked, even how long it took to put on and take off the shirt. But for a few brief moments, I had the undivided attention of another person. How often do any of us—adults and children alike—experience this throughout the course of a normal day? Yet, as Ute asked us later, does dressing a child with care and respect take any longer than reading a picture book? Interestingly, in some exercises, in which Ute timed how long it actually took to complete an act in a hurry versus in a slow and careful manner, we discovered that the hurried approach often took the same amount of time, or longer, than did the careful, focused one. This was in spite of the perceived feeling of time being sped up or slowed down depending on the mood the caregiver conveyed. In cases where the slowed approach did take longer, it was usually a matter of mere seconds "saved."

Another exercise that was partly observational and partly experiential further illustrated how important the dressing process can be. Our group sat in a circle on folding chairs as our instructors, Ute Strub and Jane Swain, associate director of the training course at Sophia's Hearth, came into the room. These two women—usually warm, calm, and attentive—were engaged in an intense conversation with each other and did not greet the rest of us. Carrying an armload of hats in their hands, they started pulling them randomly over people's heads and barking commands at each other without a word to the rest of us. It was almost as if they were racing to see who could get hats on heads faster. They slammed hats down on heads and indiscriminately yanked them off again. Our group soon dissolved into fits of laughter—the scene was just so ridiculous. But I think the laughter covered up some discomfort too. I still have an image of a participant sitting across from me, the wool edge of a hat pulled down to her nose. She looked helpless. Normally, of course, we would not treat another adult so disrespectfully. Yet I know that I have walked up behind my toddler and hurriedly plopped her hat on her head without warning. In those moments, she is certainly helpless, and I am being disrespectful. I was fortunate to start my training at Sophia's Hearth before the births of my two young children, so I not only knew about the importance of respectful and cooperative caregiving, I also had the support to make mistakes. We are not aiming for perfection, my instructors have assured me, just for greater awareness.

In a different context, the hat exercise could be jarring, conjuring painful memories of having once received careless caregiving, or eliciting intense feelings of guilt over thoughtless parenting moments. Accordingly, Ute felt that the hat exercise could be too painful for parents, and asked that we not share this particular exercise with them. (The shirt exercise, however, may be appropriate to use with parents in a parent evening, depending on the circumstances.)

These two exercises led our group to a deeper understanding of the importance of cooperative caregiving. Some of us were able to see immediate changes that we could make in our own caregiving. For example, during hand-washing time in her parent-child classes, a fellow participant now pays careful attention to children's sleeves:

> I always take my time in helping the children pull up their sleeves to wash their hands, if they need help. I encourage them to do it themselves, but if they need a hand (sometimes the cuffs are tight or buttoned), I go slowly. Sometimes a child will look at me during this time in a way that lets me know she feels cared for in that moment, and I feel so grateful for my attention having been brought to this small act through the training. I could picture myself otherwise being too "efficient"—push, push, there you go.

It's a seemingly minor change to make, but it comes with great benefits not only for the child, but also for the caregiver who has made a deeper connection with the child—it's a partnership, after all. My own experience as awkward caregiver left me humbled yet grateful. I realized that while I may feel comfortable dressing my children, dressing someone for the first time needs to be handled very delicately. And yet, in saying this, while the bond that develops over time between child and parent or caregiver is a large part of the process, in a way, we also might consider meeting the child we are caring for as if each time is the first time. As a parent and educator, I was again reminded of why I value the Waldorf and Pikler approaches to working with young children. A seemingly mundane task like dressing a small child is, in fact, a sacred act. The perfectionist in me could be paralyzed by this responsibility, but instead I try to remember that when I was receiving care during this exercise, what I needed was not for my partner to be perfect, but simply present.

These experiential exercises in cooperative caregiving gave us a tremendous opportunity for self-knowledge, but more importantly, they allowed us to feel genuine empathy for the very young child. At the same time, it can be too easy to project our own thoughts and feelings indiscriminately onto young children. The complex and varied reactions our group had to the exercises reminded us that each child is unique, an individual separate from ourselves. Caring for a very young child can be a daunting task. When I find myself feeling overwhelmed, I remind myself of a fellow training course participant's favorite mantra: "Plenty of time. Plenty of care." These are the words that allow me to step out of the shoes of the harried caregiver and into those of the child. And then I recall a shirt draped carefully over my shoulders, a hand that held mine gently, and buttons slowly buttoned, one at a time.

Kristin Fiegl is a graduate of the training course on The Child in the First Three Years at Sophia's Hearth Family Center, Keene, NH, and serves both as the facilitator of parent-child classes and as parent coordinator for the Lakeside Preschool in Essex, NY. She lives with her husband and two children in the Adirondack Mountains of upstate New York.

What's All the Talking About?

by Kim Lewis

To one who lovingly can dwell on speech

Speech will accord

Its inner light

So I will turn my heart and mind

Toward the soul

And spirit of words.

—Rudolf Steiner, from *The Genius of Language: Observations for Teachers*

When we talk with children, what is truly essential? In answering this question, a good starting place is listening, because to listen is to be present, pause, collect oneself and offer time and attention to the other person. When the other person is a little child, we may not be used to practicing the art of listening. Too often we find ourselves "talking at" the child, allowing our attention to wander, or overlooking the child's response because it may not be verbal. Perhaps sensitive listening is the secret to conversing with small children. Rudolf Steiner, in "The Recovery of the Living Source of Speech," spoke about how speech today has become deadened.[1] What can we do to wake up language in ourselves and thereby impart the living word to our children? Can the way we speak and listen breathe life into the sacred art of conversation?

As Waldorf early childhood educators delve into the work of caring for children at younger and younger ages, many are finding inspiration not only in the insights of Rudolf Steiner, but also in the practical guidelines of Emmi Pikler, the Hungarian pediatrician, and Magda Gerber, who brought Pikler's work to the United States. The Pikler approach to talking to infants and toddlers during caregiving tasks such as bathing, feeding and diapering helps forge close bonds between infant and adult. Gerber's way of speaking to toddlers in an understanding, affirming manner instills confidence and regard for others.

Talking to the child is essential for language acquisition. Learning language is an astonishing feat for the child, perhaps the greatest accomplishment in a lifetime. The process seems almost magical, full of complexities and surprises, fueled by the striving for connection with another human being. Contemporary linguists Noam Chomsky and Charles Yang believe that children are "hardwired" for learning language.[2] According to their research, children do not need to be taught how to talk; they merely need exposure to the spoken word. "Language learning is remarkably resilient," says Yang. "All you need to do is talk to children…and biology will take care of the rest."[3] As easy as this seems, the importance of speaking and listening can't be overstated, because to acquire language children are utterly dependent upon us.

Pre-verbal infants are thoroughly engaged in learning how to work the organs of speech. Talking with them assists them in their efforts. Babies move their lips, tongues, mouths and jaws when they babble and play with sounds. In watching the movements of speaking adults, babies develop "mouth-to-sound maps" from which they can actually lip-read. The child learns to make the sounds of language by imitating speech formation in adults. The speech organs configure differently to make every wondrous sound. What a gift to the observing child for an adult to demonstrate the workings of these physical mechanisms!

This exposure to adult speech is necessary for brain development. In his lecture, "Origins of Speech and Language," Steiner describes how the mental activity of perceiving and imitating the adult's movements of the mouth, teeth, lips and tongue shapes and sculpts the baby's brain. He means this quite literally. "As the infant gradually learns to speak…small whorls develop here (in the left-brain). They continue to form in an artful way."[4] The child's brain, he says, doesn't shape itself; it is shaped under the external influence of adult speech.

While talking to the child may be all that is needed from the standpoint of pure language acquisition, the approaches advocated by Pikler, Gerber, and Waldorf educators are concerned with the overall development of the child, including physical, socio-emotional and cognitive domains. And each has much to say about the nature and quality of communication. In his lecture, "Walking, Speaking, Thinking: Milestones in the Life of the Young Child," Rudolf Steiner says, "In assisting [children] in learning to speak, we need to be inwardly quite true. Life's greatest untruths are created while the child is learning to speak, since the truth of speech is taken in through the physical organism."[5] Therefore, while it is important that we talk to infants and very young children, it is equally important that we are thoughtful about what we say and how we use speech to communicate.

1   Rudolf Steiner, "The Recovery of the Living Source of Speech," lecture given in Dornach on April 13, 1923. Viewed at http://wn.rsarchive.org/Lectures/Dates/19230413p01.html (no page numbers).

2   Noam Chomsky is an American linguist credited with the theory of *generative grammar*, one of the most significant contributions to the field of linguistics in the twentieth century.

3   Charles Yang, *The Infinite Gift: How Children Learn and Unlearn the Languages of the World* (New York, NY: Scribner, 2006), p. 90.

4   Rudolf Steiner, "The Origin of Speech and Language," lecture given in Dornach on August 2, 1922. Viewed at http://wn.rsarchive.org/Lectures/OriLan_index.html (no page numbers). Also included in *Lectures to the Workers: The Human Being in Body, Soul and Spirit* (New York: Anthroposophic Press, 1989).

5   Rudolf Steiner, *Rhythms of Learning* (Hudson, NY: Anthroposophic Press, 1998), p. 106.

At the Pikler Institute in Budapest, which serves babies and young children in foster care, the nurses, as the caregivers are called, learn how to speak to the child during care activities. Throughout feeding, diapering, dressing, bathing and preparing for sleep, the caregiver is intentional and purposeful in both her gesture and speech. She draws near to the baby and makes eye contact. She announces what she is going to do before she does it, often presenting a visual cue, as well. She makes verbal requests and elicits the child's cooperation. She takes notice, mentions the happenings of the moment and follows the child's interests. With each simple sentence, she waits for the child to respond—whether verbally or non-verbally—to her words and gestures before continuing on. These are the listening pauses that create true conversation.

A typical interaction while preparing the baby for a bath might sound like this: "I'd like to take your sock off now. This is the one, here (*gesture, touch*). Can you lift your foot? (*Wait*.) Yes, here is your sock. I am pulling it off. Can you pull on it? (Pause.) You can pull, too. We are doing this together. (*Pause*.) You found a bow on your sock. It's a little bow. I see it, too. (*Wait*.) May I have your sock now? (*Child teases and keeps sock*.) That's a funny game you're playing. (*Wait*.) I'll take it now. (*Wait until child offers the sock*.) Shall we go on? (*Wait*.) I'd like to take off your other sock (*gesture, touch*)." One of the most striking impressions one gets from the Pikler videos is of the musicality or prosody of the caregiver's voice. Her gentle, melodious speech can visibly calm and delight the child.

When all goes well, these caring conversations build a healthy relationship between child and caregiver. Through early conversational models, the templates are created upon which all further relationships will be built. These care-giving encounters become sacred, protected moments in which love, warmth, and intimacy are assured. Another value of this approach is the rich linguistic nourishment it offers through language variety—that is, statements, questions, requests, encouragement, suggestions and even silliness. Since language is embedded in the *activity* of the moment, it is awakened by the act of attending to what is going on now.

Speaking consciously and deliberately about what is going on is also a wonderful tool to help the caregiver stay present. It heightens her awareness of herself and what she is doing with the child. It aids her in staying organized and focused on the task at hand. It slows her movements down, enabling her to resist the impulse to hurry to the next task. To those who observe the care-giving encounter, and to the speaker herself, the talking confirms that this child matters—she is capable, worthy of time and attention and is indeed communicating, even if she is not yet able to speak. In early infancy, babies communicate through body language, facial expression, gesture, crying and other first sounds. The sensitive caregiver recognizes these ways of relating and develops an appreciation for the baby's individual style and nature.

I recently read a story in *Educaring*, the newsletter for Resources for Infant Educarers (RIE), Gerber's California-based organization.[6] It described an older brother who grew up regularly exposed to this type of care-giving conversation between his mother and baby sister. This experience contributed to a relationship in which the boy treated his sister warmly and with high regard, valuing

---

6   Deborah Greenwald, "Beyond RIE: Observing One Older Child Respect His Younger Sibling." *Educaring* (Vol. 27, No. 1, Winter 2006/Spring 2007), p. 4.

her ideas and opinions. Also, older siblings have been known to intervene with reflective words of caution for the little one, such as, "There's the edge of the stair," stemming from their own RIE-based care. Imagine the ripple effect throughout families, communities and the world if children everywhere were bathed in the reverential words of their caregivers.

The Pikler method of speaking is also valuable because it promotes a healthy sense of "we-ness" (intersubjective awareness) and "you-ness" (interobjective awareness). Both advance the child's emotional capacities and strongly affect right brain development. We-ness is developed through togetherness, mutual understanding and reciprocity. The experience of you-ness is promoted by the child and caregiver imitating one another and matching behaviors, including vocal tone, rhythm, duration, feeling and intensity. Each partner's response is a gift to the other; each adds novelty for the other's pleasure. With the aim of gaining awareness of the child through mutual engagement, the caregiver's repertoire may include little songs, verses, games and spontaneous language as a joyful relationship is created. These positive early interactions build the child's coping mechanisms, develop self-regulation, and form positive self-concepts. They also lead to greater consideration of others in relationship.

Unfortunately, if attentive care giving wanes and the interaction between child and caregiver lapses into habit, the caregiver's words may sound rehearsed or unattached. Anna Tardos, the director of the Pikler Institute, pointed this out after our class watched a video in which the caregiver changed a child's diaper with impeccable Pikler-style verbalizations. I was impressed, but Anna explained that something was missing. What was missing, it turns out, was the *listening*. The caregiver must consider the infant every step of the way, adjusting her pace and rhythm to build rapport with the infant. Listening makes it possible to fully respond to the infant's interests and cues and match the child in tone or prosody. The relationship has to be founded on true two-way communication, making use of devices such as reciprocal, playful teasing. The interaction in the video lacked the naturalness, joy and laughter intrinsic to successful attachment, which is much more than the simple physical bond created through contact with an adult who may or may not be attentive to a child. Securely attached relationships are facilitated through liberal face-to-face contact and the gentle, loving and attentive use of words.

Talking with toddlers who are just beginning to learn the social graces of human interaction can help them gain gradual competence within their social environments. This is the case in the RIE parent-child guidance classes taught in and around Los Angeles, where the class facilitator uses a speaking strategy known by various names: "RIE-speak," "say-what-you-see," "announcing," "reporting," or often, "sports-casting," the term Gerber used.[7] Informed by sensitive observation, the facilitator will sometimes describe to the children in simple language exactly what she sees happening and what she is going to do next, allowing the children time to respond. Gerber called this response time "tarry time."

---

7   Although classes are highly concentrated in the Los Angeles area, they are also taught in Colorado, Florida, New York and Canada.

The facilitator typically illustrates RIE-speak to parents with interactions that lean toward conflict resolution. This is because conflict-free play does not elicit much verbal response from adults in a RIE class. Children are left alone when absorbed in play, as is the ideal in Waldorf early childhood settings, since independent exploration is encouraged. Children making eye contact with a parent or facilitator are generally responded to with anything from returned eye contact, to a nod of the head, or an actual acknowledgement (not praise) of what the child's process of exploration or discovery is at the moment.

In a situation in which two children both want the same object, the RIE facilitator might say, "Chris, I see you struggling with the ball. I'm moving closer to you (moving in). Sue is reaching for the ball and you are holding it very tight." The incident might end there, with proximity and validation of the experience being enough to ease the situation. Or if the conflict escalates, the facilitator might say, "You are both pulling the ball. Sue, I won't let you pull on Chris's body to get the ball." The RIE facilitator is careful to refrain from providing a solution. The children almost always walk away from the object of contention and begin another activity.

Sometimes the facilitator finds it necessary to intercept a difficult situation. She lets the children know what's coming. She might say, "Chris, I'm going to move you back a little. Sue is pushing you away. You are too close to her (pausing for a response). Here you go. I'm moving you. Sue is watching us (pause). Now you aren't so close."

In another situation, the facilitator might assist a child in reading another child's body language or gesture: "Joan! You hit Charles on the head with a peg. See. He is moving away from you. He didn't like it. If you want to hit something with the peg, you may, but Charles needs to be touched gently."

Occasionally, the parent or facilitator will want to make a comment during a child's focused play, using the same "say what you see" approach, especially if the child seeks engagement with the adult through eye contact or other means: "I see you wrapping the baby in a blanket. The baby is bundled up. Now you are patting the baby and singing a song." The adult typically does not make suggestions or try to steer the child's play in a new direction.

Some early childhood educators find what they perceive as the "constant chatter" of the RIE approach to contain too much explaining and to be "too much in the head." As described above, however, talking in a RIE class is concerned with reporting on the activity of the moment rather than on ideas or concepts.

Significant is what *isn't* said in a RIE class. Pedantic explanations and verbal interruptions are conspicuously missing, as are judging and labeling. Distracting and redirecting the child are also discouraged. There is no praising, criticizing or suggesting how the children are supposed to play. Dictates such as "you must share" or "take turns" are absent. Requests to "say you're sorry" or "say hello" are soundly avoided. Feelings are calmly and empathetically reflected, rather than explained or explored. RIE classes are often quiet and typically peaceful. Parents usually sit in silent observation for twenty minutes or more during class. As Waldorf parent-child class facilitators receive more practical training in how to talk and how not to talk to the very young, I believe the RIE/Pikler influences will be increasingly felt.

Often I observe parents new to both RIE and Waldorf parent-child classes who look for the "teachable moments," thereby intellectualizing their speech. They haven't yet been encouraged to wait patiently for the unfolding of their child's cognitive capacities, fearing instead that these capacities will not develop normally without explicit and detailed guidance. Hoping to give the child an intellectual and social boost, they direct, teach, dictate, and interrupt. I find that such behaviors can prematurely awaken the child, as well as stifle initiative-taking, and indeed they are avoided by both RIE and Waldorf instructors. Magda Gerber helped parents resist these urges by structuring classes around a "demonstrator" who interacted with the children, while the parents observed from the periphery. Gerber asked them to sit back and "do less" so they could "enjoy more."

How well does this "reporting" approach work? When I was assisting the instructor of a RIE fundamentals class last summer, the instructor wanted the adult students to experience how it feels to have another person "report" on their play. Assuming the role of "reporter," I wove in and out of the students who were busily at play with the toys they had selected. I spent a few moments with each, "reporting" what I saw. In the discussion that followed, the students were split, some finding my "reporting" simplistic and annoying, others finding it comforting and validating.

The deciding factor was how well I "listened." Listening meant being sensitive to their cues and understanding what they meant. It mattered how well I reflected my understanding back to them. When I "got it right," the students were grateful and joyful for the attention and shared experience. When I "got it wrong," they felt belittled, misunderstood and distracted by my presence. In most cases, I was able to connect with the students through verbalizations about their play. One misfire on my part involved a student who was experimenting with the sounds that rings were making as she swirled them in a bowl. I kept referring to the number of rings. ("You're swirling a ring in the bowl. Now you've put two more in.") A more perceptive verbalization would have been, "What a lot of noise you are making. Every time you add a ring, the sound changes. You're making the sound change." Another student was noticeably frustrated with my comments as she kept pointing to the baby doll ("You are pointing to her finger. You are pointing to her knee") until I finally figured out that she was showing me where the doll's skin was dirty. ("You are pointing to the places that are dirty.") Then— connection! She was noticeably relieved. This exercise helped us all to experience more directly what a toddler might feel in response to adult talk. Sensitive observation and affirming words—and refraining from presuming too much or projecting one's own ideas—are important if the child is to learn how to be in healthy, connected relationships with others.

In 1919 Steiner gave a course for teachers, translated in English as *Study of Man* and more recently as *The Foundations of Human Experience*.[8] In Lecture XI, he reveals the most characteristic feature of human development up to the change of teeth: the child is an imitative being, actively imitating everything going on around him. Steiner describes how the child is able to do this. As the child's "head spirit" is still asleep during this phase, the child remains "outside his head" among the people and activities in the surrounding environment. "Because of this," says Steiner, "the child is an imitative being."[9] He continues to say that as educators, we have no access to what is asleep, but we do have access to the wide-awake will of the child.

8   Rudolf Steiner, *Study of Man* (London: Rudolf Steiner Press, 1966), pp. 152-153.

9   Ibid.

Except in early babyhood, when the child's will is reached through the miracle of mother's milk, Steiner points us to language as the means of awakening the sleeping head spirit through the will. "The genius of language is truly gifted," he says. "It is cleverer than we are…we can work upon [the child's] sleeping spirit simply through the very first words we say for him to repeat." The movement and activity of language afford direct access to the will: "What we release in the vocal organs through these first words will penetrate the sleeping head spirit as an activity of will, and will arouse it." Early childhood educators have a responsibility to use language consciously to help awaken the spirit during the child's earliest development. But it is important that the language we use with young children stay rooted in the here-and-now, which is where the will is active, and not extend too soon into the realm of concepts and abstractions.

I find it personally helpful in my work with children to remind myself of Steiner's suggestion that our speech be "quickened with immediate present life."[10] Emmi Pikler and Magda Gerber have given us the gift of a practical approach to this "quickening" of language. Using their methods, we can learn to awaken our speech through sustained, joyful interest in the child, attention flowing from love and devotion, focus on the will activity of the present moment, and speaking the truth out of sensitive observation. A direct result of the RIE and Pikler work is greater consciousness about how we talk and listen to little children. By setting aside time, paying attention, becoming fully engaged with the children in our care, and allowing them the freedom to be who they are, we can pave the way for a lifetime of healthy, satisfying human relationships.

❧

Kim Lewis has been studying the methods of Emmi Pikler and Magda Gerber for the past seven years, after being introduced to them during her Waldorf training with Susan Weber at Antioch University New England. She has completed two trainings in Budapest at the Pikler Institute and three levels of RIE trainings in Los Angeles. She is currently living in Tucson, Arizona, where she teaches in a public Waldorf kindergarten. Kim holds a master's degree in Waldorf early childhood education.

10   Rudolf Steiner, "The Recovery of the Living Source of Speech," ibid.

Making Peace with Toddler Conflict

by Trice Atchison

Conflict is inherently distressing for all but the thickest-skinned among us. And, yet, there is a subset of people who seem, in contrast, to be enlivened by conflict. Perhaps humanity can achieve a healthy balance—one that can be learned beginning in early childhood—in which conflict is neither eschewed nor ignited, but is instead met with understanding and finesse. In this article, I hope to shed some light on this age-old challenge and, perhaps, offer some tools that may help us and our children deal more successfully with this inevitable aspect of life.

A typical progression for new parents: We have a child, and our hearts are melted. We're vulnerable, and so is our newborn. We try our best to shelter this innocent child, who grows fast and soon becomes a part of the wider world. We bring him to a playgroup, the park or a library read-along. The other new parents seem friendly enough, if also a little nervous, and the children happily observe and participate in the activities. This is healthy, this is good, this is peace, this is community.

And then a little boy, not more than two and for no apparent reason, reaches out to pull a tuft of our own child's hair. Hard! Unprovoked! Our child yells in protest. We are shocked and dismayed. This is not what we had in mind. We want a perfect, conflict-free world for our deeply loved child. No hair pulling, no hitting, no teasing, no excluding! These thoughts cloud the present moment, and we lose all perspective.

Fledgling parents often seek a utopian experience for their child, and this can be especially true among parents drawn to Waldorf education. Many parents speak of the visceral reaction they had the first time they ever walked into a Waldorf early childhood classroom—the peach-blossom lazured walls, the simple cloth dolls and wooden toys, the fresh flowers on the seasonal table, and the smell of bread baking in the oven. Parents rejoice: *This is it! I've found a Garden of Eden for my child.*

I, too, was enthralled with the goodness and beauty I sensed the first time I entered a Waldorf nursery, and knew that this was the setting I wanted for my child. I still hold these positive views about a form of education that is healing, inspiring, developmentally appropriate and joyful. The difference now is that I know from experience that conflict and struggle also occur within those pastel-colored walls. We are, after all, still here on Earth.

Utopia is not ideal

As parents, we can strive to offer our children valuable experiences we may have enjoyed, or missed, as children, but we cannot surround them with perfect harmony. Even if we could achieve this end, we would not be serving our child's best interests. As Barbara Ehrensaft says in *Spoiling Childhood: How Well-Meaning Parents Are Giving Children Too Much, But Not What They Need*, "In human relationships, the act of reparation, making good on something that did not initially go well, is far better for character building than providing our children with a conflict-free, idyllic, 'perfect' childhood."[1] Sometimes there's trouble in paradise. What's more, this trouble is normal, and a valuable learning experience for all of us as we help children navigate their way through conflict. To do this, we must become more aware of the feelings and preconceptions we bring to conflicts that we and our children encounter, and strive to be more objective and present in regard to whatever manifests in the moment.

Certain trends in parenting can make this objectivity toward and acceptance of conflict all the more difficult to achieve. These trends include: the blurring of boundaries between parent and child, especially common during the early years; an overzealous desire on the part of parents to offer their children an "optimal" childhood; and an overblown fear of conflict of any kind in the name of peace. In these ways, parents may be hampering their children in learning how to co-exist with others. As teachers and parents, we can help children build character and important life skills by accepting conflict ourselves as a normal part of toddlerhood, childhood and adult life. As psychoanalyst and pediatrician D.W. Winnicott said, "If society is in danger, it is not because of man's aggressiveness, but because of the repression of personal aggressiveness in individuals."[2] In other words, an extreme aversion to, and lack of acceptance of, aggression as part of life—and a corresponding inability to address conflict—can actually lead to distorted forms of aggression that can harm individuals, families and the whole social fabric. Further, the lack of authenticity that accompanies this denial of aggression can result in children and adults who suffer from depression, anxiety and other ailments. We had better get a handle on this natural phenomenon, so that our classrooms and communities are not filled with children whose well-meaning parents and teachers are unwittingly creating turmoil, as with the child, Richard, described here:

> *Pamela and Gordon believed that a crying child meant a failing parent. As a small baby, their son, Richard, was given a warm and enriched environment. He had two parents who anticipated his every need and quietly removed obstacles from his course before he ever knew they were in his way...He had a bucolic and blissful first couple of years...His parents remained attuned to his every need. Richard smiled most of the time...*

---

1   Barbara Ehrensaft, *Spoiling Childhood: How Well-Meaning Parents Are Giving Children Too Much—But Not What They Need* (New York: The Guilford Press, 1997), p. 238.

2   Ibid, p.187.

But then it was time for Richard to attend preschool. Nirvana quickly turned to purgatory. Pamela and Gordon [had] failed to present their son with the 'gradual failures' that would allow him to function in the world….[Richard's] conflict-free home life existed in stark contrast to his new battlefield at school. Soon the battles were carried home…In the concerted effort to keep Richard satisfied and gratified, Richard was deprived of the basic tools that would help him cope in the world—patience, waiting his turn, dealing with frustration, problem solving, hoping for something better.[3]

The unhappy situation described above begins in infancy, with the parents quietly clearing Richard's path of all obstacles. He never has to experience frustration or exert himself to solve a problem on his own—even one as simple as retrieving a toy he has flung out of reach. This practice starkly contrasts with the RIE (Resources for Infant Educarers) approach to young children, which discourages parents and caregivers from intervening too soon in a misguided effort to smooth a baby's path of obstacles. As RIE founder Magda Gerber writes in *Your Self-Confident Baby: How to encourage your child's natural abilities—from the very start*, "To respect your child is to create a little distance so that you refrain from interfering with her experience of encountering life…RIE's respectful approach encourages a child's authenticity, or genuineness."[4]

In this light, creating a frustration-free environment for a young child can be viewed as a form of disrespect—one that alienates the child from her truest self. Of course we are meant to protect and nurture our young children; but when we strive for the impossible goal of eliminating even small upsets and challenges—wanting everything to be easy and happy all the time—we can create a sense of helplessness in the child that keeps her from developing confidence in her own strength and emerging abilities. This sense of helplessness can cast a veil of uncertainty over her interactions with life, and is, in fact, an untrue assessment of all she really is capable of doing.

Approaches to addressing conflict among children

Waldorf early childhood teachers have often successfully used redirection as an approach to resolving conflicts among children. When Sally and Sammy are each insisting on using a child's broom at the same time, the teacher might get the dustpan and brush and show one of the children how to sweep up the dirt. Or she may encourage Sammy to bake some muffins in the play kitchen. This occurs without a long speech about the importance of sharing, or a dictate that each child must take a turn of a certain length with the broom before switching. Sarah Baldwin, author of *Nurturing Children and Families: One Model of a Parent/Child Program in a Waldorf School*, specifically reminds parents to be aware that children this young often simply cannot share, and recommends that parents and teachers work together to redirect children.[5]

---

3   Ibid, pp. 163-164.

4   Magda Gerber, *Your Self-Confident Baby: How to encourage your child's natural abilities—from the very start* (New York: John Wiley and Sons, Inc., 1998), pp. 3-4.

5   Sarah Baldwin, *Nurturing Children and Families: One Model of a Parent/Child Program in a Waldorf School* (Spring Valley, NY: Waldorf Early Childhood Association of North America, 2004), p. 89.

The strong, healthy daily rhythm of a Waldorf classroom can do much to help prevent or minimize conflicts. The rhythm helps children to know what to expect, to transition smoothly from one activity to the next, and to avoid becoming over-stimulated or bored (conditions that can prompt conflict). Waldorf early childhood teacher Barbara Patterson, in *Beyond the Rainbow Bridge: Nurturing our Children from Birth to Seven*, says, "Like a heartbeat or the rising and setting of the sun, our classroom rhythms hold children in a secure balance. Our outer activity comes to meet whatever wells up within the children as we move through repetitive daily and weekly rhythms."[6] The flow of activities each day is carefully thought out to allow for a natural "breathing in" and "breathing out" of focus and energy. Ronald G. Morrish, author of *Secrets of Discipline: 12 Keys for Raising Responsible Children*, supports this practice. He describes the need for children to have a healthy dose of rhythm and routine in their lives in order to avoid feeling off-balance and unharmonious: "These days, many [children] have to think their way through every part of the day. Many parents no longer stress routines and nothing is predictable. Children have to stay alert and deal with constant change...Too often, we forget that children struggle to get through days like this the same as we do. They also become agitated, irritable and unproductive."[7]

Additional wise strategies effective in minimizing conflict include a hearty mid-morning snack (heading off problems that can arise from simple hunger), and encouraging early bedtimes and daily naps to help ensure that children are well-rested. It is up to us as adults to create an atmosphere that, as far as possible, fosters peace and purposefulness—and, of course, to model peace ourselves. It is not helpful to toddlers or to children of any age to be placed in situations that cause undue stress and confusion, in which the children never know what to expect. A well-rested, well-fed, assured and engaged child will tend to play well by herself and co-exist well with others. But, as we know, even in such positive circumstances, conflicts crop up. Children also bring with them varying levels of coping skills from day to day; these can be due to simple overtiredness or other temporary factors, constitutional differences, and issues children may be absorbing from their family life, such as parents' marital difficulties or job pressures.

Patterson suggests various options for dealing with aggression and conflict when they occur in the classroom:

> *A child who bites can be given a large piece of apple or carrot and must sit beside the teacher to eat it. "We bite the carrot, not our friends." For a child who scratches, bring out the healing basket and trim the child's nails. "Kittens scratch, but not children." A child who spits may be taken to the bathroom to spit into the toilet.*[8]

---

6   Barbara Patterson and Pamela Bradley, *Beyond the Rainbow Bridge: Nurturing our children from birth to seven* (Amesbury, MA: Michaelmas Press, 2000), p. 119.

7   Ronald G. Morrish, *Secrets of Discipline for Parents and Teachers: Twelve keys for raising responsible children* (Fonthill, Canada: Woodstream Publishing, 1999), p. 57-58.

8   Patterson and Bradley, p. 119.

Patterson also recommends listening carefully to children as they describe what happened in a conflict with another child, noting that a child who feels sincerely heard seems better able to let go of the conflict and move on. She also helps children struggling to enter social play in finding creative ways to become involved, increasing the chances that the other children will respond favorably to a new playmate. For example, a child of kindergarten age might be encouraged to knock on a neighbor's "door," basket in hand, to say that she's having visitors for tea and would like to borrow some dishes, as opposed to crashing in on the dish hoarders, accusing them of being unfair.[9]

RIE practitioners advocate more specifically and directly guiding children engaged in conflict. First, however, children must have a chance to work out conflicts on their own—with just enough adult help as is needed to lead them through an impasse. In this way (as with the infant trying to reach a toy on his own) children's capabilities and competence are acknowledged as they gradually gain mastery in dealing with their physical world and social relationships. Gerber says:

> I believe in letting children struggle over a toy as long as neither one is getting hurt or hasn't reached a point where he is past his limit of coping with the situation. Struggle is part of life, all aspects of life. There is a famous Hungarian stage play called The Tragedy of Man. In one scene God looks down and speaks to Adam and Eve, saying, "Struggle and keep hoping."[10]

Gerber's words bring to mind images of a woman laboring through childbirth, a chick pecking its way out of a shell, a sperm's journey during conception—all examples of rich and necessary struggle.

A helpful learning tool from RIE

A RIE-based article by Denise Da Ros and Beverly Kovach, "Assisting Toddlers and Caregivers During Conflict Resolutions: Interactions That Promote Socialization," offers specific guidelines for caregivers in dealing with toddler conflict and in exploring one's own inner response to conflict in terms of how it might influence the way a caregiver chooses to intervene.[11] The first step is quiet observation, maintaining an open and nonjudgmental attitude. Moving in close to the conflict and remaining at the children's eye level, the caregiver watches and waits, unless, of course, a child's safety is at stake (all the while ready to intercept any hitting gesture). The caregiver may then describe to the children what she sees ("I see that you have the sheep, Thomas, and that Sarah wants it, too."). The caregiver, curbing her desire to quickly solve the problem out of a need to erase her own discomfort, waits to see whether the children, thus acknowledged, still need to struggle. She offers just enough involvement, if any, to help the children solve the problem themselves. Often the simple act of moving in close, or of simply stating to the children what is happening, is enough to dispel the conflict. The caregiver stays nearby until the conflict is resolved, remaining available to comfort either child, and modeling gentleness toward both the "aggressor" and the "victim" (she does not actually view

9   Patterson and Bradley, p. 119.

10 Gerber, p. 188-189.

11 Denise A. Da Ros and Beverly A. Kovach, "Assisting Toddlers and Caregivers During Conflict Resolutions: Interactions that Promote Socialization." *Childhood Education* (Fall, 1998, Vol. 75, No. 1), p. 29.

the children in terms of these limiting labels). The caregiver continues to verbalize what she sees happening until the toddlers disengage.[12] Da Ros and Kovach conclude that "Adults' ways of relating and responding during toddler conflict will affect the immediate outcome of toddler problem-solving. When and how much adults should intervene, and the kinds of strategy they select, will affect the authenticity and competence of the toddlers who are in the adult's care."[13]

As Gerber, with her customary common sense, states, "If either child's emotions reach the boiling point and his behavior falls apart, or either child is intent on engaging in aggressively hurtful behavior like hitting or biting, you may decide to separate them. You can say, 'I don't want either of you to get hurt, and it looks like one of you might. I'm going to separate you now.' "[14]

The Da Ros and Kovach article was especially helpful to me in practically dealing with classroom conflicts that occurred during parent-toddler classes I have taught at the Great Barrington Rudolf Steiner School. In classes that consist of up to eight parent-toddler pairs each day, with children ages one-and-a-half to four, conflict sometimes arises. In preparation for writing this article, I practiced the steps outlined above, and also took a closer look at my own deep discomfort with conflict, and with the mistaken idea that, ideally, there *wouldn't* be any in the classroom, or that a "good teacher" knows how to remove conflict in a snap. The insight to see conflicts as necessary and educational—and to question the wisdom of desiring an entirely conflict-free environment—helped me to become more effective in assisting the children and parents.

Practical applications

At the initial signs of conflict, I would move in closer. When warranted, I "reported" to the children, in simple language, what I saw. I was amazed at how affirming and calming these steps could be for the children. The feeling of "Ah, she understands," was palpable. At times, redirection still felt like the more appropriate response for such young children—but I also could more clearly observe how parents' overly enthusiastic attempts at redirection often backfired and, indeed, did not adequately acknowledge the child's feelings of frustration, inevitably leading to further frustration and conflict. (Perhaps the child thinks, "Why is she asking me to make muffins? Can't she see that I really want that broom?!") With empathy, I also was able to observe how uncomfortable some of the parents were with conflict in the classroom, particularly when their own child was involved in it.

I began to tell "victims," in a matter-of-fact manner, that they could say "No," or "I don't like that," when another child was invading their space. Years ago, I read a magazine article by a rape survivor who wrote about having been raised to be a "good girl" who never said no or wished to hurt anybody's feelings by refuting them, setting limits, or "making a stink." These learned habits of so-called "niceness" were the conditions that led to her rape. This harkens back to Gerber's goal of authenticity. It is simply false, unnatural, and even dangerous to smile apologetically and remain accommodating when someone is violating your personal space.

---

12   Ibid.

13   Ibid., p. 30.

14   Gerber, p. 190.

I wrote a letter on the topic of toddler conflict to the parents, and gave them a copy of the Da Ros and Kovach article. The parents joked good-naturedly when I mentioned the topic, "Oh, toddler conflict, we don't know *anything* about that!" Over the next weeks I saw the parents (and myself) develop greater comfort and skill in observing conflicts in process, allowing them some time to be resolved, and quietly acknowledging what was transpiring when a conflict was in effect. Of course, the children and parents were also by this time more familiar with me, each other, the classroom and our rhythm, but even considering these other factors, happy, peaceful play clearly increased as the weeks went on, in part due to the new awareness the adults were bringing to the classroom. Together we strived to refrain from distracting a child away from a conflict too soon or from trying to make the children "happy" by swooping in with a ready solution. If I noticed trouble escalating while I was busy with snack preparations and parents were occupied with their craft and conversation, I could say, "I think the children in the play kitchen may need to have an adult nearby," and one of the parents would get up, move in close, and be ready to respond or intervene as needed. Conflicts occurred less frequently in the final weeks, and there were no longer any full-blown struggles. A number of parents commented on how helpful they found the letter and article to be.

It's interesting to note that when spouses or other caregivers (such as a grandmother or nanny) would occasionally accompany a child to class in place of the parent who came regularly (and, therefore, was more likely to have read previous hand-outs), the more typical approach to conflicts began to be more noticeable to me. These strategies included trying to quickly solve the problem for the child, seeing one child as the aggressor, the other as the victim, or trying to "jolly" the child out of her frustration. The contrast in approaches indicated that we really had managed to begin changing the general classroom culture in this regard, with occasional lapses into old patterns. The group had, by this time, more information on the topic of toddler conflict and regular practice with our new approach.

RIE's emphasis on asking adults to notice and explore their own feelings and responses—while simultaneously keeping them in check—is key to this process. In short, allowing the conflicts to occur with less parental and teacher discomfort and less quick intervention, and verbalizing problems as they occurred, had the effect of noticeably increasing peaceful play within the classroom over time.

This "sports-casting" to the children differs from the traditional Waldorf approach, in which the teacher is urged to speak less and model more, to quietly and "behind the scenes" create a healing and peaceful environment, to indirectly address certain themes through story-telling and puppetry, and to show the children more acceptable ways to interact. However, my own direct experience and observations with the RIE approach to toddler conflict, as well as the parents' positive remarks and follow-through, convince me of its worth and appropriateness within the classroom, in addition to the more traditional, and deeply valuable, approaches to conflict within a Waldorf early childhood classroom.

Overcoming our "harmony addiction"

Kim Payne—a psychologist and former Waldorf teacher who lectures worldwide on parenting, education and social issues—is opening new areas of inquiry within Waldorf schools by encouraging a more direct approach to conflicts among children of all ages. During a lecture entitled "When Push Comes to Love: How to Raise Civilized Children in an Uncivilized World," Payne said: "As adults, we need to get over our 'harmony addiction' and develop policies both at home and at school for dealing with conflict in a more straightforward way."[15] He, too, urges us to embrace conflict—not to immediately separate children when they are arguing, but to help them work it out so that they can develop a sense of who they are in relation to others.

Sharifa Oppenheimer is another advocate for teaching children conflict resolution skills. In her book, *Heaven on Earth: A Handbook for Parents of Young Children*, she says, "It will require us to take our own emotions in hand and work with ourselves, not only to model justice, but also to shed light on human dynamics and creative problem-solving at an early age… [When guiding children,] there are three essential elements to remember. 1) Use the same tone of voice you use for 'here's the towel.' Simple, informative, clear. 2) Rarely is there a situation in which there is a true 'victim' and 'aggressor.' There are two sides to every child's disagreement, and you need to know both. 3) Keep it simple. A few words used skillfully are far more effective than the best lecture on justice and equality."[16]

My interest in how to handle toddler conflict has prompted me to begin studying the topic of conflict resolution more generally, and to engage in a more in-depth exploration of my own knee-jerk reactions to, and feelings about, conflict. Toward this end, *Nonviolent Communication: A Language of Life*, by Marshall B. Rosenberg, is a valuable book that could have remarkably healing effects on individuals, families and organizations taking up the practices it outlines. The language and communication skills described are meant to strengthen our ability to remain open, human, authentic and responsive even in challenging situations. Rosenberg prompts us to abandon our habits of blaming, judging, retreating, threatening and pigeon-holing. Instead, he invites us to compassionately work our way through conflicts by observing our feelings, realizing our needs and calmly making requests. His nonviolent communication process (NVC) has been used with much success in situations ranging from family and relationship problems, to community-wide conflicts, to political strife on a global scale.[17] The steps Rosenberg outlines can feel stilted and scripted at first, but, honestly, the world could use a helping hand in the form of a beginning script as we all gain practice with new and healthier ways of relating.

15 Kim Payne, "When Push Comes to Love: How to Raise Civilized Children in an Uncivilized World." Viewed at http://www.thechildtoday.org/Articles/

16 Sharifa Oppenheimer, *Heaven on Earth: A Handbook for Parents of Young Children* (Hudson, NY: SteinerBooks, 2006), p. 202.

17 Marshall Rosenberg, *Nonviolent Communication: A Language of Life* (Encinitas, CA: PuddleDancer Press, 2005), p. 8.

Hope for the future

As Morrish wrote, "A few years from now, our children will be in charge of our country and our communities… They will be responsible for looking after the environment, preventing wars, and educating a new generation of children. How well our children do in the years to come will, to a great extent, be determined by how well we raise them now."[18]

Our own discomfort with conflict and desire to squelch it can have a profound ripple effect into the future, leading to more complex problems. Like the children who have the potential to grow through conflict, if we let them, we all can benefit from learning the tools that lead to conflict resolution. With practice, we can become worthy examples to our own children, to the children in our classrooms and their parents, and to our communities—as we learn to make peace with conflict.

∾

Trice Atchison teaches parent-child classes at the Great Barrington Rudolf Steiner School in the Berkshires region of Massachusetts, where she lives with her husband and two boys. She is a graduate of the training course, The Child and Family in the First Three Years, at Sophia's Hearth Family Center in Keene, NH, She holds a master's degree in writing and publishing from Emerson College, Boston, MA, a bachelor's degree in philosophy, psychology and art from Wheaton College, Norton, MA, and is a freelance writer and editor.

18   Morrish, p. 141.

Tending and Cherishing the Living Spiritual Forces in Childhood

by Joyce Gallardo

Entering the room where a newborn baby lies is like entering a serene temple. A delicate fragrance fills the air, and the whole room feels bathed in a sense of peace that inspires our reverence and awe. In the presence of this mystery of new life, we may ponder the question: From where do these fresh, vitalizing forces come that radiate through the infant and through every young child in the earliest years of his life?

A majestic panorama of this phenomenon has been painted by Rudolf Steiner, who has said that the child we see before us during the first three years of life is fundamentally different from the one who is there later on, for during these early years the most sublime forces are active in the child. These are the very same forces, he says, that once streamed through the body of Jesus of Nazareth at the baptism in the River Jordan, when the cosmic Christ descended and indwelt a human body for three years.[1] In Steiner's view, these forces are not associated with traditional Christianity; rather, they are a universal reality available to all.[2] These same vitalizing spiritual forces—if they are tended and cherished in early childhood so that they may remain flexible and fresh throughout life—contain the promise of awakening in each individual the virtues of brotherhood, reverence, love, compassion, forgiveness, tolerance, and sacrifice.

---

1   Rudolf Steiner, "The Work of the Ego in Childhood, A contribution towards an understanding of the Christ," lecture given in Zurich, Switzerland, February 25, 1911. Published in *Anthroposophical Quarterly* (21:4, Winter 1976), p. 90.

2   Steiner points out that all of the ancient spiritual streams were aware of what he called the Sun Being, or Christ, approaching the earth. "Even if there were no human being who knew anything about the name of Christ…we do not overstress the importance of names—what is all-important is the *Being* Himself… What matters to us is the reality, not the name." (From Steiner, "The Work of the Ego in Childhood," p. 91.) Throughout the ages, this Sun Being has been known by many names: in India as Vishva Karma, in Persia as Ahura Mazdao, in Judaism as Yahweh, in Egypt as Ra, whose representative on earth was Osiris. He was known as Apollo to the Greeks, Taita Inti to the Incans of South America, and to the Hopis of North America, Tallawa.

The formative forces active in every young child lay the foundation for spiritual awakening in adulthood, Steiner says. As adults, however, we must strive consciously to gain access to the realm in which little children are unconsciously immersed. "Our whole life must, therefore, be dedicated to the transformation of what is present within us during the first years of childhood."[3] This knowledge can inspire those of us who care for young children to further deepen our understanding of the profound nature of early childhood and of how we might best nurture and support the child during the first three years of life.

Emergence of the I

In "The Work of the Ego in Childhood," Rudolf Steiner says that recognition of the "I" awakens in the child at about age three, but that the Ego is nonetheless present during the first three years of life. The Ego, the child's true being or individuality, lives in the soul, yet the child is not aware of it until the age of three. During the first years of childhood the Ego is very active, elaborating and molding the brain into the delicately complicated structure it is to become. In its artistry, the Ego is guided by higher spiritual beings whose forces stream into the child. Steiner has said, "During these years the human skull is still pliable and the spirit is still able to work in it. Later on this close connection ceases; the 'I' experiences itself in the nerves and can therefore become conscious of its own existence."[4]

It is a momentous experience when for the first time a child refers to himself as "I." The German poet Jean Paul, in his autobiography, wrote of the birth of his self-consciousness and recognition of his essential selfhood as an "occurrence taking place only in the veiled holy of holies of a human being," for this "I" is the very child himself—his eternal essence.

Karl König, in his book *Eternal Childhood*, gives us a moving picture of this moment:

The moment the child uses the word "I," he has become an inhabitant of the earth. This moment, which happens in the life of every human being, is a critical point in human development, and so is one of the most difficult events in a child's life, a cross-roads at which many children falter and perish. Many autistic and psychopathic children break down at this particular point. First, they shrink back, and then they withdraw into themselves and cease to communicate with the surrounding world. They generally regress, beginning to wet and soil themselves again and stop playing and talking. Such a condition occurs when, unconsciously, of course, the question "Who am I?" profoundly shakes the child's entire existence. Especially during this particular time the child needs a lot of understanding, guidance and fellowship.[5]

Protecting the vitalizing forces

The question arises for us as caregivers of young children, "How do we tend and cherish these life-giving forces during the early years so that the child, once grown, can still draw on them?" We

---

3   Steiner, "The Work of the Ego in Childhood," p. 91.

4   Ibid., p. 88.

5   Karl König, *Eternal Childhood* (Botton, UK: Camphill Press, 1994), p. 124.

understand the baby as a totality of body, life forces, soul and spirit. How important is the care of his body, which bears the living formative forces and the imprint of the spirit! Being in the presence of a newborn baby illuminates these truths of earliest childhood and helps transform them into a living experience.

The nerve-sense system of the infant especially requires our utmost care and protection. Dr. Wilhelm zur Linden writes in *A Child is Born* about the vital importance of the early sense impressions a child receives:

> *[The infant's] soul enters right into every organ and limb of the body. Thus the soul and spirit receive sense impressions very intensely at this age, though not fully consciously. The organs are formed in their finest structure with the help of these sense impressions. As the sense organs develop, so the soul awakens with the help of the impressions of touch received through the nerves all over the skin, the impressions of light, the effects of warmth and cold, the sound of speech and song, noises of all kinds, the taste of food, and the love or lack of it of those around him.*
>
> *This shows how vitally important it is to present the infant only with carefully selected healthy sense impressions. For it is at this early stage that his sense organs find shape and [the] basis of health which will be [his] for life. And the sensitivity of the soul, which is fed by the senses, depends on their delicacy or coarseness.*[6]

Dr. zur Linden is referring to the bodily senses, of which there are four—the sense of life, the sense of touch, the sense of self-movement, and the sense of balance or equilibrium. In light of what we know of the living spiritual forces in the child in the early years, we then approach the bodily care of the child with the deepest respect and reverential devotion.

Dr. Henning Köhler, in *Working With Anxious, Nervous, and Depressed Children*, points out that the sense organs serve us like vessels in which the inflowing of the outer world undergoes a kind of higher chemical process. In the "vessel forming" of early childhood, the angel of the child longs to enable him to form ideals and become capable of moral fantasy. The angel strives to pour impulses of love into the soul of the child. Through nourishment and healthy development of the four lower senses a vessel is created for later achievement of "genuine social participation and possible selflessness in a person's awareness of her fellow-human beings, sensitizing her to others' way of speaking and thinking and to her perception of their unique individuality."[7]

Care of the senses

Several years ago Dr. Michaela Glöckler—from the Medical Section at the Goetheanum in Switzerland—gave a talk on the dignity of the young child at a conference of the Waldorf Early Childhood Association of North America, in which she spoke of caring for the infant's senses. Dr. Glöckler said that eighty percent of humanity suffers through life with a sickened, limited sense of self

---

6 Wilhelm zur Linden, *A Child is Born: Pregnancy, Birth and First Childhood* (London: Rudolf Steiner Press, 1973), pp. 70, 80.

7 Henning Köhler, *Working with Anxious, Nervous and Depressed Children, A Spiritual Perspective to Guide Parents* (Fair Oaks, CA: AWSNA Publications, 2001), p. 22.

(a damaged life sense) and that the other twenty percent can give themselves in service to the others. Thus, she said, the *new culture of humanity* is dependent upon a strong, healthy sense of self. She added, "One capacity that compensates for every incapacity is love."

Köhler calls the life sense the *fundamental sense*. Rudolf Steiner once described this sense as a state of "feeling comforted and comfortable through and through," of being at home in oneself as a fundamental orientation toward life. All other later orientations build on this. Our self-confidence and trust in existence depend upon the state of inner restfulness, self-containment and security that comes from a healthy life sense.

In *Eternal Childhood*, König described the "primordial trust" that lives in the child:

The soul-being of the child is characterized by the primordial trust which accompanies the path of the newborn from a higher world into the world of body and senses. The newborn soul unfolds if the human environment approaches it with love, warmth and care... This "primordial trust" is (or is not) confirmed by the bodily sense experience during the first months after birth.[8]

A sense of being sheltered, protected, and stable provides the foundation on which a child may develop self-confidence and trust in existence. How is this sense of shelter and comfort conveyed? Through tender care and gentle touch, and by handling the child in a mood of unhurried peacefulness and love. (We communicate something of our own essence to the child by our touch.) It is preferable that the child be kept in a horizontal position when held; being put into a vertical position too soon has an overly stimulating effect on the baby. We create a sheath of comfort and protection for the child by dressing him in soft layers of natural fiber clothing and swaddling him in the protective cocoon of a warm blanket. By covering his head with a hood or cap we protect the fontanel, into which is streaming the living spirit. The budding sense of life is thus nurtured when we help the child experience goodness as a bodily condition. It is from a bodily basis—for it is all developed out of our bodily nature—that we come to an awareness of the Spirit.

A living model of sensitive care

A living model for this tender quality of caregiving is found at the Pikler Institute (also known as Lóczy), a residential home for children in Budapest, Hungary, founded by pediatrician Emmi Pikler in 1946 after World War II had left many children orphaned.[9] Based on her work and research as a family pediatrician, Dr. Pikler set up an educational process which would promote healthy development for a child living in an institution. She knew that the maternal relationship could not be reproduced in an institution like Lóczy, yet she was certain that it was possible, within a community framework, to offer young children the possibility of establishing warm relationships with their caregivers. She herself trained the nurses at Lóczy to care for children with respect, gentleness, quiet devotion, and with inner participation. Love, based on knowledge of the child gained through observation, is the guiding principle that informs the Pikler approach. The unfolding of each individual child is cherished and respected.

8   Karl König, ibid., p. 93.

9   The Pikler Institute is also a center for research and training, with students and observers coming from all over the world.

Reverent, cooperative, face-to-face caregiving is the norm at Lóczy, where every physical contact is preceded by a gentle verbal and visual cue for the child. Emmi Pikler said that the baby needs the "word" of the adult, especially in the absence of the mother, and that the child should be "bathed in the words of the caregiver." Further, she encouraged the involvement of the child in all care activities, to allow him to become an *active participant* rather than a *passive recipient*.

The slow, deliberate movements of the caregiver and the beauty of her gestures reflect her inner participation. While observing at Lóczy, I saw a nurse tenderly applying oil on a cotton ball to the creases of a baby's body, hands and feet after his bath. Anna Tardos, director of the Pikler Institute, and daughter of Emmi Pikler, remarked, "She is anointing the child, as Mary Magdalene anointed the feet of Jesus." This remark underscores the depth of reverence with which care is provided at Lóczy, even though the Pikler approach does not articulate nor work from a defined spiritual perspective. The caregiver's finely developed higher, social senses engage with the child's lower, bodily senses of life and touch. Her soothing voice, soft eyes and sensitive hands create a reverential atmosphere.

A video about Lóczy shows a three-week-old baby who had been brought from the hospital where her mother had abandoned her. The clothes the baby was wearing had to be returned to the hospital, and so the head nurse undressed the newborn slowly and tenderly, and spoke comfortingly as she leaned in close to the child. The baby took in the mood of the adult, sensing her quiet hands and inner attitude of compassion. The infant's tense little body relaxed under the touch of the nurse, whose every gesture was meant to ease the pain of the loss of this child's birth mother. Such exquisite bodily care nurtures the life and touch senses of the infant, and the process of healing can begin.

Welcoming the newborn

The newborn wants to sleep all the time because, as Steiner describes it, he is not yet at home with us on the earth, and in sleep he can return to the comfort of the spiritual home from whence he came. He has to gradually grow into his physical body. Emmi Pikler also recognized the child's struggle to feel at home in his body:

> In the beginning, the child feels more or less uneasy during the care situation. Often he doesn't like it, he cries, wants his peace and quiet… If, from the start, we handle an infant peacefully, patiently and carefully, he will discover ever more joy in these activities, learning at the same time to trust us more and more, and to take an increasing part in our work.[10]

Since the babies at Lóczy are bottle-fed, great care is taken to feed them in the same order each day, with undivided, focused attention. During feeding, the nurse holds the child in her arms at a forty-five degree angle, called the "Madonna position" by Magda Gerber, who founded Resources for Infant Educarers (RIE), based on Pikler's insights. If another child cries during feeding, the caregiver will say soothingly, "I know you are hungry, but I am feeding Catarina now and I will feed you next." I witnessed at Lóczy how the lilting, comforting sound of the caregiver's voice helped soothe a crying infant as he waited his turn to be fed.

---

10   Emmi Pikler, *Peaceful Babies, Contented Mothers*, sixth edition (Budapest: Medicina, 1963).

There is a rhythm to all that the caregiver does, day after day, week after week, which has a supportive effect on the maturing life sense. With the bath, also, the child knows just what to expect as the caregiver bathes each part of his body in the same order each day. Bedtimes in the evening and naps during the day are regular and consistent. The children's daily life is peaceful, stable and predictable; it flows like a gently moving stream from one activity to the next, with rest and sleep in between. This is especially important for the children of Lóczy, many of whom have experienced early lives that consisted of fragmented, disconnected events. The rhythmical care they receive gives them the sense of security they need to experience their ongoing development.

Respect for self-mastery

Another important aspect of the care given at Lóczy is respect for the self-initiated, independent movement of each child. The children I observed there were steady and sure on their feet—graceful and agile in their movement and play. No child is put into a position until he tries it himself. The adults do not "teach" the infants. They do not decide what babies need to know or when they should turn over or sit up. Careful attention is paid to the infant's own self-initiated activity, for if this goes unrecognized, the child becomes dependent upon the adult for support in learning motor skills and loses the capacity for self-reliance. Dr. Pikler noted that the child's transitional postures, from supine to turning onto the stomach, stretching and rolling, creeping on the stomach to crawling on hands and knees, are critical in the development of later motor capacities. She recognized the children's joy in harmonious movement.

With the kicking of the feet, the turning of the head, the grasping with the hands, we see the manner in which the child's will awakens. Here we have a picture of the child's inner initiative. Rudolf Steiner said that we would feel great reverence if we would observe a child first kicking his legs awkwardly in every direction and then watch as he gradually learned to control himself. He said, "It is quite wonderful to discover in the child's single movements, in its search for a state of equilibrium, the terrestrial after-effects of those heavenly movements executed in a purely spiritual sense, as spirit among spirits."[11] All the more reason to adapt an attitude of non-interference in regard to the child's attempts at movement in the early years. This attitude is present at Lóczy.

Karl König illuminates the sense of movement with these words: "The sense of movement gives the child a feeling of freedom in his soul. More and more skills are acquired in cooperation with the sense of movement, and when the soul is alive in the unfolding of its motor abilities and skills, then the feeling of joy penetrates it. Joy is nourished by the sense of movement."[12]

We have all witnessed the joy of a child left free to move on his own, without interference or "help" from adults, a joy reflected in the radiance of his smile. Encountering the children in our care with an open, radiant smile encourages the kindling of joy in their souls and helps in the awakening of their sense of movement.

---

11   Rudolf Steiner, *Man's Being, His Destiny and World Evolution* (Spring Valley, NY: Anthroposophic Press, 1966), p. 35.

12   Karl König, *A Living Physiology* (UK: TWT Publications, Ltd, 1999), p. 205.

Supporting the higher capacities of humanity

Nurturing the child's four lower senses of life, touch, movement, and balance is important on many levels. Steiner articulated that the sphere of sensory experience is part of the path to the higher self, and the physical senses provide the right milieu for the maturing of the higher social and spiritual senses. For example, the sense of touch is fertile ground for development of the sense of the Ego of another (for perceiving the other's individuality), while the sense of life relates to one's ability to perceive the truth or falsehood in the thought or concept of another. It is possible, if we engage our life sense and concept sense, to listen *behind* the words of another, and there meet the Spirit of Humanity who lives in the child in the first three years of his life.[13] The sense of movement is essential for the development of one's own speech and the sense of others' speech, the capacity to discern how others express the Spirit through speech. Balance and inner calm are preconditions for development of the sense of hearing.

Capacities from the feelings transmitted by the senses reappear on the soul level. From the feeling of well-being transmitted by the life sense comes a capacity for patience and reverence, which lays the foundation for the social virtue of tolerance. Respect, unhurried peacefulness, and patience are essential qualities of healthy human relationships. In being tolerant with others, we leave them free to be themselves, while we take an unprejudiced interest in their uniqueness. This takes a certain degree of selflessness, but we cannot achieve that degree of altruism without a firm sense of self born of a healthy life sense. Köhler says, "If the 'open secret' of the life sense were to be widely enough discussed and practically applied as a matter of course to educational directives, we would be laying at least the tendency to *cultivate tolerance in every baby's cradle.*"[14]

The sense of touch is the seed-source of caring concern in our approach to life, which when it is refined can also be described as the social attitude of brotherly love. In his documentary, *Lóczy, A Place to Grow*, French filmmaker Bernard Martino gave a commentary of his observation of the social attitude, which he called "brotherhood," that was alive in the children at Lóczy.

Rudolf Steiner has said, "Without the sense of touch, man would have no feeling of God. What permeates everything, what permeates us ourselves, what holds and carries everyone, this all-permeating divine substance, enters consciousness and is the inwardly reflected experience of the sense of touch."[15]

Through the sense of movement we experience freedom of soul and through the sense of balance we have a sense of inner rest. A capacity for compassion and the sense of justice are the two moral-social capacities related to the motion- and balance-sense complex, just as tolerance and caring are related to the life- and touch-sense complex. Köhler refers to these four aspects as what is embedded in the phrase, "love of one's neighbor."

---

13   Albert Soesman, *Our Twelve Senses, Wellsprings of the Soul*, (Stroud, UK: Hawthorn Press, 1990), p. 128.

14   Köhler, ibid., p. 39. Italics as in the original.

15   Rudolf Steiner, "Man's Twelve Senses in Their Relation to Imagination, Inspiration, and Intuition," lecture given in Dornach, Switzerland, August 8, 1920. Published in *Anthroposophical Review* (Vol. 3, No. 2, Summer 1981), p. 17.

Beacons of light

These sublime ideas can be beacons of light for those working with young children. Many feel a real sense of urgency in this work, much of which must be therapeutic, bringing healing where it is so needed. Yet, one cannot help but ask: If a heightened sense of the importance of protecting the bodily senses in infancy were the norm in our culture, would so many children, adolescents and adults be in such desperate need of healing?

More and more children are coming to us with damaged lower senses. "To be born is a hazardous undertaking. The incarnating soul is exposed to the arbitrary decisions and impulses of human beings who have ample scientific information on the physiological processes of birth yet may lack understanding of the deep issues involved. Many no longer possess the instinctive wisdom of their forebears."[16] Our culture assaults the budding senses of the young child in so many ways—early exposure to media, arrhythmical home lives, inadequate warmth, to name a few. Improper diet, irregular sleeping habits, too-early awakening of the intellect, and an underlying, pervasive feeling of fear within our culture all create conditions counterproductive of healthy growth and development.

Many of us are involved with the care of infants and young children in daycare centers and home care settings or within our own families. We have been given the special task of caring for these babies during the most vulnerable time of their lives. Others are offering pre-natal classes, parenting classes or parent-child groups, creating a place of sanctuary in these times. As we begin to experience these spirit-filled thoughts as living realities, they can become a guiding star, a spiritual foundation on which to build our relationship with each child in our care.

Can we begin to find ways to nurture, support and empower women and their families, both during pregnancy and after giving birth, with these lofty, yet eminently practical, thoughts? How can families provide a healthy, nurturing and protective environment that is mutually nourishing for the mother and her newborn child? Perhaps even before conception we can be instrumental in helping soon-to-be parents prepare themselves to receive their newborn child with a knowledge of, and reverence for, where their baby comes from and what he profoundly needs from those who will care for him. Parents are finding their way to us for a reason—it may be their unborn children who are guiding them.

The task is monumental, but if taken up, in Köhler's words, "with courage born of insight," we can provide the support and encouragement parents need to come to a deeper awareness of the significance that protecting the bodily senses of the infant at the beginning of life has for the whole of life. This knowledge, received with open mind and heart by parents, can inspire the awakening of the selfless devotedness of will needed to tend and cherish the living spiritual forces that are present in their children during the first three years.

☙

16 Stanley Drake, *The Path to Birth* (Edinburgh: Floris Books, 1979), back cover.

Author's note: The theme of tending and cherishing became even more poignant for me when, while writing this article, I learned that my daughter was expecting a child. Our family was blessed with the arrival of Katary Alexander on December 13, 2007. Soon after he was born, I held him in my arms, a little piece of heaven. What a special time of the year in which to be born, when the spiritual world is preparing once again for the birth of the Christ Child—that Sun Being—and when one senses how "angels from the realms of glory wing their flight o'er all the earth."

Being in the presence of a newborn baby during the Holy Nights has illuminated these truths of earliest childhood for me and helped to transform them into a living reality. It was a most precious gift while writing this piece to participate in the daily rhythm of enfolding, protecting and nurturing our baby grandson and his mother and to see them both thrive in the light and warmth of the love that permeates their surroundings.

Joyce Gallardo is a member of WECAN'S RIE/Pikler research group. She has been a kindergarten teacher for more than twenty-five years and is the director of Los Amiguitos, a family day care home, offering a Waldorf nursery and kindergarten program. She has taught kindergarten, high school Spanish, and calligraphy at Hawthorne Valley School in Ghent, NY. Joyce is currently training in Spacial Dynamics.

Working with Parents

Building Bridges: How Infant-Child Classes Can Help Support Families

by Donna Stusser

Attention is powerful when it comes to parenting. The following story—a vignette from a parent-child class for babies at the Summerfield Waldorf School in Santa Rosa, California—illustrates the beauty and power of paying attention.

Our parent-child groups consist of up to six families—mothers, fathers and their babies ranging in age from three to seven months. The babies develop quite dramatically over the course of the few months we meet. They change from quietly cooing on blankets to noticing one another. Some of the older babies soon crawl across the room to seek out a toy held by another. They almost always enter the classroom with a big smile on their faces and quickly get down to the business of playing with the toys and exploring their surroundings.

One of the goals of my work in teaching these classes is to provide an atmosphere that supports infants in discovering the magic and joy of being in a physical body on their own. In time they master basic movement patterns and learn to feel confident moving around on the floor with ease and flexibility.

Quiet attention

A key component of the class is observation time. These times for careful observation are inspired by the work of infant educator Magda Gerber, founder of RIE (Resources for Infant Educarers), who was, in turn, inspired by the Hungarian pediatrician Emmi Pikler. Many of Rudolf Steiner's indications for the healthy, unhampered development of babies mesh gracefully with the Gerber/Pikler approach.

Children love to feel the quiet attention of their parents. During observation time we try not to chat but, rather, to focus on what we see. For example, if a baby has rolled over, we notice how his hands are placed in front of him, how after a few minutes his fingers unfold from a fist to raying out. We notice what his eyes might be looking at, and how every so often he tucks his chin in towards his chest. The same baby, on his back now, might reach for his toes and pull on his sock. We see so much as we observe, and also notice how easily we miss a movement progression in one baby while focusing on another. This process of observation is much like a muscle we work with each week.

During observation time, the babies are free to move on their own. Therefore, it is helpful if they begin from a position they can move in and out of freely. For instance, if a baby has only rolled over onto her tummy once, then she would be placed on her back at the start of the observation time. Similarly, if a child has not yet mastered getting into and out of the sitting position, we begin where the child is most comfortable independently.

Ely's story

When a new session started up that included continuing families and new arrivals, I suggested to a new couple, Jina and Tom, that when they felt ready they could allow their baby boy to lie on a blanket next to them. They willingly gave it a try, but Ely was not so comfortable on the floor. My heart reached out to him in his frustration; I had seen this situation before. Ely arched his back, squished up his face and protested with a squawk of distress. "Up!" he was saying to his parents through his baby language.

Jina commented that Ely didn't like to be on his back. I hoped that over the next few weeks I could gently guide the parents toward helping their son discover the magic that can happen for a baby on the floor.

I suggested to the parents that they try small doses of back lying when Ely was well-rested and happy. I encouraged them to lie right down there next to him, to play with him in bed, and to allow him to lie on their bodies. I also encouraged them not to prop Ely in a seated position, since this too-early taste of uprightness was keeping him from enjoying his rightful time in a prone position.

During week two, excitement filled the air as we settled into class. I asked all of the parents to reintroduce themselves and their children. Jina, Tom and Ely were last in the circle of five families to speak, and during the series of introductions, Ely lay happily on the floor, squealing joyfully. Jina described to the group what a week it had been! She and Tom told us that Ely had been in the Intensive Care Unit after his birth, and during this time they had learned infant massage. They now decided to incorporate infant massage into Ely's floor time. Tom, who was temporarily off work, recovering from knee surgery, found that the floor was the most comfortable place to be—so both father and child would have their "floor time" together. When Ely would begin to express his discomfort, Tom would apply a gentle massage technique, such as joint compression or simple holding. I believe that the deep witnessing by his father that Ely experienced during these times helped the child sink more comfortably into his body.

Ely changed dramatically over the weeks. He no longer had such a strong need to be "entertained." He quickly moved through movement patterns on the floor. He rolled from back to front, and then began to push up on the floor with his toes and feet so that he was doing, in essence, the "downward facing dog" yogic pose. Every time I observed him, he appeared busy and occupied with a new discovery. We were all so delighted, especially Ely. He was discovering the joy of movement and how to use his body to further his discoveries. He was the initiator and the master of his movement, and his determination and mastery increased along with his obvious delight in himself.

From entertainment to self-mastery

Ely's story is unusual in some respects, due to the struggles of his early days. Because of a compromised respiratory system, he received a monthly visit from a nurse after he was able to go home from the hospital. During the visits, the nurse suggested to Jina that she try to get Ely to move more. They would then roll him back and forth in a blanket, stretch out his arms in front of him when prone, and place him in positions he couldn't get into himself. As a result, Ely's playtime evolved into a time in which others played with him and tried to get him to move in ways he didn't especially want to. Ely was unhappy both lying on his back and on his tummy. As time went on, Ely's parents placed him in a walker-like piece of baby equipment (but without wheels) in which he could sit upright and play with toys. He liked this position, and Jina received encouragement from the nurse to continue to sit him up, although he was not yet ready to do so by himself. Once he got a taste of the world from that perspective, he would scream even louder when placed on the floor. His well-meaning parents concluded that he "just didn't like it," and Ely spent many hours in his favorite contraption.

Looking at Ely's situation, we see that from his earliest days what could have been quiet playtime, exploring the possibilities for movement and discovery, became an exercise in externally defined, goal-oriented contortions and manipulations. This lack of quiet playtime also meant that the parents never received a much-needed break from the direct care of their new baby—a baby who had experienced a rough start. Each parent felt that there was something they should be *doing* to help him along, and the nurse corroborated this outlook.

Then they found their way to an infant class in which they could witness other babies exploring at their own pace and in their own time. This inspired them to aid Ely in becoming more comfortable in his body—which, ironically, meant returning him to the dreaded back-lying position. But this return allowed him to go back and move in a sequence that was natural for him, allowing him to master essential back-lying movements before progressing further. By observing both Ely and other infants, Jina and Tom gained the confidence to allow Ely to have this experience and remained committed to letting him discover how to move on his own.

Jina beautifully expresses her realization about how healing floor time can be: "[Ely's] movements became his own. He began to have reasons to move. In retrospect, I now realize that I should have waited for him to be comfortable and never have moved his arms or helped him roll. There is no way I will be moving him to learn his movements again. It creates a kind of splintered learning with no other purpose but to succeed in a task at hand that has no meaning for him."

This family's story is unique in that the time it took Ely to grow comfortable in his movements on the floor was greatly reduced due to the extra healing touch of his father and the particular dedication of both parents to support their son. Nonetheless, in ten years of engaging in this work with infants, I have witnessed other families who faced similar challenges and who grew to see their children's struggles in a new light.

Filling the well

Parents everywhere want their children to be happy and content, and often are willing to jump through hoops to make this happen. At the same time, parents want some moments to themselves to get things done or to replenish themselves so that they can continue giving to their children. This is one of the main reasons why parents who thought they would never use the television as a "plug-in-babysitter" succumb to placing their children in front of the set. "I will be such a better parent if I get some time to myself," they say, or, "It is just so that I can get this place cleaned up."

But if we assist our children, from the earliest ages, in discovering self-directed play and entertainment, both parent and child can "fill the well" so that they can be both together and apart more joyfully. While it is valuable for parents and their children to share pleasurable moments together, I don't feel it is the parents' responsibility to entertain their baby. Rather, it is our responsibility to provide the environment in which infants can safely and contentedly learn. This brings us back to observation.

A little bit of letting go

Taking the time to give our attention to our children builds a bond in a different way than does holding and touch—although cuddling is, of course, wonderful and essential, too. But if the baby feels seen and appreciated, she can then feel content to be on her own for a time. For a newborn, this might be ten minutes twice a day with the parent close by. An active nine-month-old baby may be able to play for half an hour three times a day in a safe space while the parent cooks a meal or does some floor stretches of her own.

Babies can feel when we observe them without an agenda, simply open with our interest and attention. They need a measure of this kind of quiet, connected attention in order to happily become absorbed in their own explorations later on. Witnessing our children's glorious moments of discovery, as well as their frustrated struggles, aids us in seeing them as growing individuals. A bridge of connection between parent and child is built through direct contact, close observation and a little bit of letting go.

※

Author's note: When my first child was six months old, I received a visit from Birthe Kaarsholm, an old friend from my years in Sacramento who had studied Goethean Science and the fine art of observing phenomena in the natural world, and who later deepened her studies to encompass a lifelong passion for movement. Birthe introduced me to the concept of allowing babies to move on their own as freely and naturally as possible, and of closely observing this process. She also introduced me to the work of Emmi Pikler and Magda Gerber, the movement work of Bonnie Bainbridge Cohen, and to Body-Mind Centering. A window into my future opened up. I am eternally grateful to Birthe for helping me to see the possibilities for integrated movement in babies. We continue to study together the phenomenon of how all movement affects babies—how we move around them, how we move them, and how they move.

Donna Stusser has been facilitating parent-child classes at Summerfield Waldorf School for six years. She completed her Waldorf early childhood teacher training in Sacramento, California, A Course in Babies with Hari Grebler in Santa Monica, and courses in infant and child development at Sophia's Hearth Family Center in New Hampshire. She lives with her husband and two daughters in the country near Sebastopol, California.

A Gradual Transition to the Nursery

by Marilyn Pelrine and Kirsten Carr

For the very youngest children, the shift from home life to a nursery program is a momentous, and sometimes difficult, transition. At The Waldorf School in Lexington, Massachusetts, the Buttercups Transitional Nursery—which has an extended transition time built into it—helps ease the journey into school life, allowing young children to gradually and gently discover the joy of being together with other children, without their parents present.

The innovative program for children ages two-years-and-nine-months to three-and-a-half is an option for families who wish to avoid an abrupt parting. Providing plenty of loving support, Buttercups acts as a welcoming bridge between our parent-child offerings and the child's first experience in a group setting on her own.

Parents remain with their child in the classroom for the first two months of the program, and then are welcomed back for special occasions later in the year. Parents also are invited to monthly evening meetings on topics of child development tailored especially to their needs and interests. The program was designed to supplement the school's well-established nursery and kindergarten programs for older children. For children who have been at home for the first few years, the gradual parting helps avoid separation issues that can derail some first nursery experiences.

Both parents and children feel more secure in a structure that supports a gradual letting go of the parent's hand, and a gentle shift to the loving hand of a familiar teacher. Many parents find the idea an attractive one. Indeed, *Boston Magazine*, in its issue on "Best Private Schools in Boston," cited this program as one that distinguishes The Waldorf School, Lexington, from other preschools.

Getting to know you...

A home visit during the summer allows children to become acquainted with their teachers in the security of their own home. Before the first day of school, we hold a picnic for families on a grassy hillside behind the school. Incoming families are welcomed and introduced, potluck fare is shared, and both parents and children have a chance to meet each other in a casual, park-like setting. This gathering also gives teachers a first view of the children as a group. As part of a school-wide "School Warming" event, an evening meeting for parents takes place before the first day of school, giving us the opportunity to discuss with parents how to ready the children and themselves for this beginning nursery experience.

The weekly schedule begins gradually, as well. In the first week we meet for one hour only. In the second week we hold class on one day for two hours. By the third week, the parents and children attend according to the normal schedule: two days, three hours each. At the beginning, our morning resembles a parent-child class. Parents are present throughout, engaged in handwork and room chores, and quietly observing. They join in with the children for kneading dough and enjoying snack, circle time and a puppet story.

During the fourth and fifth weeks, a few parents begin to step out of the room during free play while their children are happily engaged, increasing their time away to 30 minutes. By the sixth week, we encourage all parents to leave the room. In the seventh week, we have parents settle their children into the first morning activity (bread making), say goodbye, and then return in time for tidying up, snack and circle. A "goodbye window" allows the children to wave to Mom or Dad in the parking lot. This is a helpful bridging activity, and many children join in to wave to the parents of their friends. Each week thereafter, parents increase their time away from the class until all the parents have fully transitioned out of the room. Individual adjustments are made depending on each child's readiness for the separation.

At first, as parents begin to leave the room, we ask them to stay on the school grounds. On occasion a child may need to take a walk with a teacher to go find his mother. After touching base, the child usually rejoins the class in short order and with little drama. This threshold experience of the children being on their own for the full morning with the teachers in the classroom coincides with the week of the Lantern Walk festival in early November. We use a puppet story during this week that portrays the children's experience of being on their own at school and reflects the sense of gathering courage to step into the unknown—of carrying one's light out into the darkness. This story is printed and sent home for the parents to tell. In January, after a three-week break, we are always surprised at how sturdily the children reenter the class with few separation issues.

We keep parents involved with our class throughout the year. One way in which we do this is by including parents in our goodbye circle every morning. Parents arrive a few minutes before dismissal time so that they may rejoin us as we all hold hands, circle 'round and sing goodbye.

Once parents are fully transitioned out of the room, they are invited back to class for a "Parents' Tea" in February, March, April and May. The children help prepare the room for snack time on this special day, and we listen for a knock on the door. The parents join the class for snack, circle and puppet story, and stay for the rest of the special day. In this way, parents have an opportunity to witness firsthand their child's integration into the group and his or her level of comfort in being at school.

Despite this careful orchestration, there are usually one or two children who are not ready to separate. In this case, the mother stays in the room and works alongside us, but continues to leave the room gradually, according to the child's readiness. We work together with the parents to observe and assess the child's needs, creating the best transition for the child. We strive to find the right balance of offering the child a challenge without pushing her too quickly.

Watch, wait and wonder

Observation of the children is a large component of our classes. When in the classroom at the beginning of the school year, parents are encouraged to engage in purposeful work in order to free the children to enter into their play. We ask the parents to note specific aspects of child development during their observation. They are also given a simple handwork activity to work on while observing in order to busy their hands and avoid the impression of staring at the children. By participating in the observation exercise and purposeful work, parents are freed up from being overly involved with, or creating self consciousness in, the children while they play. The teachers, of course, continue to quietly observe the children throughout the year.

We introduce the parents to the following approach at the beginning of the year, and use it consistently when addressing conflict and discipline issues with the children:

Watch

Observe the children. Try to be as objective as possible. Also observe your own inner reactions to what is happening with the children, striving to suspend judgment.

Wait

Give the children some space to work out a solution on their own. If a conflict is continuing, come near to the children, holding the space, and describe in simple language what you are observing: "Johnny is pulling on the tail of the horse. Sally is pulling on the horse's head." Strive to stay in the moment without judgment. Hold the space for a moment and wait, continuing to observe the inner feelings and outer events. This process may be enough for the conflict to be resolved on its own.

Wonder

Breathing deeply, strive to be open to finding a new way of solving problems. If a conflict continues between the children, strive to use imagination and inspiration to find a solution: "The horse does not like to be pulled so hard. Let's bring him over to the barn and give him a rest." Be open to something new!

Free movement and respect for the child

The children are encouraged to move freely, on their own initiative, during free play and throughout the morning, using gross motor activities such as climbing, jumping, sliding, walking, running, pushing and pulling (as appropriate to the space and social situation). If a child is not able to do a certain activity and wants help from the parent or teacher, we wait and encourage the parents to wait, also, in order to give the child a chance to do it on her own.

We consciously speak respectfully to the children, and tell them in advance when something will be happening. Every day, we follow a familiar rhythm which provides security for the children. They know what will happen next during the school morning.

Care and attention to feeding and dressing

Eating and dressing activities are given ample time and attention during the school day. We consider the daily snack time a meal and honor the experience with a blessing and a table set with napkins and cups. We like to provide some quiet time at the table for the children to focus on the experience of eating.

While helping with dressing, we take the time to focus on each child, making eye contact, smiling and using imagination. This special time of connecting individually with the child enlivens the experience of dressing. Children are encouraged to dress on their own and their skill at being able to dress themselves increases during the year.

Social modeling

Throughout the morning we seek to model appropriate social behavior for the children. If there is a conflict, and the "Watch, Wait and Wonder" approach is not enough—for instance, the child may be upset over not getting a toy, or may be trying to grab a toy from another child—the teacher will intervene. She models the use of words such as, "You may say 'May I use the toy?' " If the child using the toy is not ready to give it up, the teacher will model a response such as, "*You* may say, 'I am still playing with the doll. You may have it when I am done.' " The teacher will then tell the first child, "You may wait," and help to redirect her to another activity. Usually, the child holding the toy will come over at a later time and give it to the one who wanted it. This social modeling seems to work well to foster genuine sharing. Forcing a child to give up a toy when he is not ready does not honor the child's needs. Respect for each other's needs and healthy boundaries are encouraged in this way, and sharing often begins to occur naturally.

Parent support

Integral to our work is parent support. We devote ourselves to guiding parents, appreciating their hard work and sharing in their struggles and joys. By supporting parents we foster secure bonds and healthy connections with their children. Healthy parenting means thriving children.

The parent work begins during the initial interview. We listen well and cover both basic and intimate topics relating to the child's first years. We observe the child and may offer a suggestion or two. Many families have been with us previously in our parent-child classes and, in these cases, support is already ongoing and a rapport has been established.

When the parents are with us during the fall, we consciously model a respectful attitude toward the children. Following the indoor observation time described above, we arrange for the parents to gather outdoors with a teacher to share their observations and reflections while the children are involved in their play. Many wonderful insights are brought up during these moments. Additionally, we are sometimes available after class for brief conversations or for a telephone conversation.

We offer two to three individual parent/teacher conferences throughout the year. In these 50-minute sessions we build a picture of the child at home and in class, discuss issues and problems, and work collaboratively and supportively. We refer parents for outside professional support as needed (occupational therapists, remedial specialists, anthroposophical doctors, and so on).

Parent evenings

We meet with the parents of Buttercups Transitional Nursery children once a month, working with the book *Beyond the Rainbow Bridge*, by Barbara Patterson. We cover seasonal topics, child development issues, and classroom updates, using a format that encourages each person's participation. Singing, handcrafts and refreshments round out our evenings. We see these meetings not only as educational, but also as providing a forum for parents to connect with each other, building community.

Handouts

Parent education is enhanced by weekly handouts that we have carefully selected. Seasonally, we include writings on the following topics: television and media, the importance of play, discipline, parent support, child development, Waldorf education, and the work of RIE (Resources for Infant Educarers) and Emmi Pikler having to do with the care of very young children. Each family receives an issue of *Renewal* (the magazine on Waldorf education published by the Association of Waldorf Schools of North America) in the fall and spring.

Our place within the Waldorf school

The first transitional nursery grew out of a need to create a stepping stone from our parent-child classes to the nursery. Having begun five years ago in a borrowed room that required daily setting up and breaking down, Buttercups is now housed in a permanent and beautiful room—visible, recognized and well-supported by the school.

The array of classes we offer for parents and children from birth to three years is embedded in a mature Waldorf school. This solid framework enables our programs to flourish. We receive administrative support (advertisement at open houses, scheduling of interviews and admission support, a direct phone extension, and so on), which allows us to put our energies into running, rather than filling, our programs.

Reciprocally, we help the school to grow. Our offerings for parents and young children are appreciated as important feeder programs for the early childhood classes and, consequently, the school as a whole. Through our commitment to parent education, parents in our classes become well-versed in the fundamentals of Waldorf education and how home life can support this. They gain a level of appreciation for Steiner's ideas about education and child development by experiencing them firsthand. Likewise, the children in our classes, familiar with the school and the Waldorf approach, adjust well into the early childhood classes and, later, into the grades.

At least half of the families in Buttercups have previously attended our parent-toddler classes, and some even began in our parent-infant classes. Indeed, a real community of parents and children forms in these early classes; they are already a cohesive group when they move on to the nursery.

Co-teaching and other staffing

There are two teachers in Buttercups and both are recognized and compensated for full-time teaching, which consists of five morning and three afternoon classes.

Each co-teacher is thoroughly invested in the work and in supporting the other, and we each feel that our individual strengths can be fully realized. We work closely with each other and put our heads together on a daily basis, strategizing and planning the details of the classes and needs of the individuals within them. We regularly review and reflect: "How might we improve the class? What small changes could we make in the schedule or in the physical surroundings to allow the class to function more smoothly?" In addition to our daily conversations, we schedule a weekly business meeting together.

We often have a third pair of hands in the classroom helping out—a volunteer or intern who commits to working with us for a minimum of several months. It can be very useful to have one more adult working consciously to promote harmony in the room.

Conclusion

For us, choosing to work with young children means working hand-in-hand with parents. With the Buttercups Transitional Nursery, the school responded to a need to create a bridge that would link the programming of one typical Waldorf program (parent-child) with another (the standard nursery, beginning at age three-and-a-half). The school was willing to offer a hybrid program, which has proven to be well-received by both parents and children, and which works well for parents able to navigate its unique time commitments. Having a number of supportive factors in place—the admissions infrastructure, the co-teaching option, and a large enough school to support such an array of early childhood offerings—makes it possible. This, along with the chance to provide an orientation that supports parents in their early years on the parenting journey, creates a fertile ground in which the program and its families can flourish.

෴

Kirsten Carr has worked at The Waldorf School in Lexington, MA, since 1998, and has a background in psychology and early childhood education. Before beginning her Waldorf teacher training, she had worked with children in a variety of settings, including a Montessori program, Children's Hospital in Boston, and with infants in a RIE daycare program.

Marilyn Pelrine has a background in elementary education and has studied birth-to-three work at Sophia's Hearth Family Center in Keene, NH. She has taught in the early childhood department of The Waldorf School, Lexington, MA—where her four grown children were educated—for 23 years.

Additional Information on the Transitional Nursery

Buttercups fits into an array of other class offerings that allow us to offer a full garden of programs for parents and young children at The Waldorf School in Lexington. Our various classes are for children from birth to three years:

Winter Park: A drop-in program for parents in the community and their children up to three years old, Winter Park is held from October to May. The program began twenty years ago as a gentle, welcoming support for mothers in the community. It is facilitated by an early childhood teacher or experienced parent in the community, and offers a less structured, informal gathering place for parents and an introduction to a Waldorf early childhood environment. There is no set fee—parents pay on a donation basis. Winter Park is often a parent's first look at a Waldorf school.

Rosebuds, for infants six weeks to ten months old (pre-walkers): These parent/infant classes, scheduled for five- or seven-week sessions, allow time for silent observation, sharing of observations, sharing from home life, singing, hand/finger play, a snack for the mothers and a lullaby to close. Weekly handouts are offered, including selections from *You are Your Child's First Teacher* by Rahima Baldwin Dancy, *Your Self-Confident Baby* and Dear Parent by Magda Gerber, and *The Baby Whisperer* by Tracey Hogg.

Roses, for babies ten to twenty months old (mobile babies): This offering for parents and young toddlers meets for sessions that are five to seven weeks long. The format is similar to that of the younger baby classes, including a snack time for all and adult discussion from the same books and handouts.

Morning Glories, for two- to three-year-olds: These parent/child classes are offered in nine- to twelve-week sessions. The format is a simpler version of the Buttercups Transitional Nursery class. Our study book is You are Your Child's First Teacher. Two parent evenings are offered each session.

Sweet Peas, for children two-and-a-half to three-and-a half years old: This is a full-year, one-day-a-week program with the same format as Buttercups, except that parents remain in the class all year. Parents have handwork projects in class to encourage the children's independence and play. Children are often shyer and younger that those ready for Buttercups. Monthly parent evenings are held.

The Buttercups Transitional Nursery is structured as follows:

9:15-10:35	Breadmaking and cleanup
10:35-10:10	Free play
10:10-10:20	Tidy up the room
10:20-10:30	Bathroom time
10:30-10:40	Circle time
10:40-11:00	Snack time
11:00-11:10	Rest time
11:10-11:20	Puppet story
11:20-11:30	Get dressed to go outside
11:30-12:15	Outdoor time

The morning begins with parents bringing the children into the room, helping them take off their outdoor clothes and find an apron, and settling the children down at the table. Parents then say goodbye to the child. Children will knead bread into shapes while the teachers are kneading bread and leading the singing. A clean-up song encourages the children to help sponge the table and sweep the floor, all the while singing. The children then begin free play. There may be several table activities available, such as building with small blocks, coloring, setting up a play scene with shells, or stringing beads. There is a lentil table, which comes out in the main play space once a week during the winter. Teachers may help facilitate the play, or mediate with the children, and imaginative, independent play is encouraged. Teachers model activities for the children throughout the day.

A flute is played to indicate tidy-up time. The teachers sing while putting away toys and engaging the children in helping. At bathroom time, all children line up, with one teacher at the head and one at the end, to walk down the hall. Later, when back in the room, a short circle follows with large motor activities, fine motor finger plays, games and songs. Children are then invited to the snack table. After a verse is sung, a reminder for "quiet bites" encourages the children to fully enjoy their food and serves as a time of in-breathing and refreshment. After ten minutes, the teachers will then tell a story at the table, and then the children are invited to share their own stories one at a time.

At the end of snack, the children clear their dishes and come to the rug for rest time. This is followed by a puppet story, with each child sitting on his own pillow. One at a time, children put their pillows away, begin to dress themselves and then are brought outside to the adjoining yard as they are ready. They enjoy outdoor time in the fenced-in garden in winter, longer walks with the parents in the fall, and springtime walks and picnics with their teachers. The morning ends at the garden gate, with a goodbye circle that includes parents.

A New Vision for Creating Partnerships with Parents

by Margaret Ris

What new mother has not felt a flush of anxiety in the first weeks after the birth of her child? She realizes that she alone carries the responsibility for keeping alive this tiny, dependent and needy newborn. Not only must she care for him now without any real experience, she must also somehow assure that he matures into a decent, contributing member of society. What a prospect! It is not uncommon for mothers to feel this anxiety deeply in the immediate postpartum period, and for fathers, too, to experience it when they recognize the awesome responsibility inherent in parenting.

As Waldorf educators working with younger children for longer periods of time than ever, and offering daycare to working parents, we carry an increasing responsibility both for the children in our care and for their parents. In years past, the teacher might receive a child no younger than age three-and-a-half or four, after parents had become more accustomed to their new role. Kindergarten generally lasted for a morning of three or four hours, as a chance to play and socialize. Programs for children are now more a family need than a pleasant option. The dynamic has changed dramatically, and so compassion and support for parents have become ever more essential ingredients to our task of caring for the children.

Helping parents discover the art of parenting

When both parents and caregivers are able to focus on what is best for the child, the child will end up with the most integrated and wholesome experience. I would recommend that early childhood teachers and care providers adopt an attitude of partnership with parents, sensitively and non-prescriptively sharing practices and insights they have learned in professional training. Perhaps as we work professionally to cultivate the *art of education* and the *art of childcare*, we can also envision helping parents discover an *art of parenting*.

Ultimately, it falls to parents to sculpt the milieu in which their child develops. The influence of the parents' backgrounds and attitudes, the kind of environment they provide, and the caregivers they select will all influence the child. It can be daunting!

One of Rudolf Steiner's key insights about the young child is that he learns primarily through imitation. Another is that the little child absorbs sensory input in fine and exquisite detail and takes these effects into his very body as well as into his developing psyche. What the child sees, hears and experiences from the earliest weeks enters deeply into his developing self.

It follows that supporting a parent to be conscious of his or her own words, attitudes and actions will supply the child with the healthiest model of imitation. Making parents aware of this, without alarming them or raising their anxiety or guilt, is a task that requires extraordinary sensitivity. Parents are simply individuals, as we all are, with strengths, weaknesses and foibles. They need not be perfect. Attachment studies have indicated that the most securely attached infants are not those whose signals were consistently picked up and attended to by the mother. Rather, children who experienced instances of disruption in communication followed by recognition and repair were more securely attached.[1,2] The process of attachment "disruption and repair" proved to encourage a certain healthy resiliency and confidence in infants. In a sense, it is as though these children were raised in a "cold hardy" atmosphere of attachment, rather than like delicate hothouse flowers in a highly controlled atmosphere. When their genuine needs, but not their every whim or whimper, were met, the children were able to encounter a greater array of responses, move through them, and experience a recurring sense of attachment after the "disruption" in communication.

The journey toward parenthood

New parents are also in a tender phase of their own adult development, and are undergoing a great deal of adjustment and learning. Supporting mothers and fathers in their experience of becoming parents—by informing, encouraging, validating, and inspiring them—can create a lasting and health-giving effect for the whole family. With intention and sensitivity, we can help parents become conscious of how to create healthy lifestyles and mutually rewarding relationships.

Parenting can indeed be a path for self-development. Just as the child learns to roll over, walk, climb, speak and sing, parents are also learning how to navigate and grow into their new roles. *The child and his or her parents are in a parallel process of self development; however, the milestones of child development are well-articulated and recognizable in comparison to the parents' less defined process of adult self-development in the role of caregiver.* Erik Erikson has identified the generative stage of adult social development as including family nurturing and career building, but writings on parental self-development are fewer.

Our love for the children in our care can expand to include love for the parents who have brought these children into life and who wish to provide them with the best possible future, although it may not be clear to them specifically how to accomplish that. Nowhere is this more important than in the earliest years, when the child is most impressionable and the parents most vulnerable.

---

1   Beatrice Beebe, "Co-Constructing Mother Infant Distress in Face to Face Interactions: Contributions of Microanalysis." *Zero to Three Journal* (May 2004), pp. 40-46.

2   E.Z. Tronick, "New thoughts on mutual regulation: co-creation and uniqueness – 2002" in *Parent–Infant Psychodynamics: Wild Things, Mirrors and Ghosts*, Joan Raphael-Leff, ed. (London: Whurr Publishers, 2003).

A continuum of approaches to parent education

As parent educators, we have a continuum of tools for working with parents, from modeling ways of being with children, to holding study groups and engaging in conversation, to outright instruction. And perhaps the most beneficial approach may be to take the stance of a helpful, but non-prescriptive, guide and supporter.

Modeling ways of working with children requires that the parent participate in a class situation to observe how a teacher/caregiver works with a child (for example, in parent-child classes, as a parent helper, or in a facilitated playgroup). Sometimes RIE (Resources for Infant Educarers) classes are formally structured as demonstrations. The teacher interacts with the children while the parents observe. Later they may discuss and process the new information and supplement the class time with readings.

Many approaches are less overt than this; teachers in a Waldorf parent-child class often use an implicit, non-verbal approach to illustrate to parents ways they can relate to their children. A parent may or may not pick up on this. If they do absorb what has been modeled, this new approach might remain on the unconscious level. Mom doesn't quite know why she has started to speak in a more soft and melodious tone with her young child; she just took it on because it seemed to work when the teacher spoke in this way. Or Dad may consciously recognize the benefit of narrating a conflict between children instead of intervening, and adopt it openly—even soliciting others to try it, too, because it worked so well in class. Or a mother or father may never pick up on the subtle approach— instead they may pass the class time in a sort of reverie, appreciating the break from solitary caregiving or the chance to chat with other parents. The modeling technique, while an optimal way to interact with and teach the young child, is not necessarily the most effective teaching tool for the adult, whose learning mode has moved well beyond the imitative stage.

On the other end of the continuum, parent education via prescriptive *instruction* takes on a more authoritative aspect, as in the case of a doctor's recommendations (for example, "I recommend you feed her rice cereal mixed with milk at six months then add pureed root vegetables twice a day"). This more formulaic, one-size-fits-all approach can breed a kind of submission to expert advice and a reliance on external versus internal decision making—or it can breed resistance and resentment. Parents in need of assurance often will gladly accept the advice of a trusted expert on physical or behavioral matters. And certain facts of child development need to be communicated to parents. But as we know, expert opinion on many childrearing practices has flip-flopped over the years, knocking the experts off their pedestals. Further, this style of parenting support can eclipse the opportunity for parents to develop their inner guidance—to become more conscious of what they are doing, to make wise choices, and to weigh the advice they receive in light of what is most appropriate for their family and lifestyle.

Today, there seems to be a call for a different path. It may be that we can best serve parents by offering *guidance* in the form of sharing ideas and by giving them opportunities to knowingly take up relevant ideas and practices of their own accord, because they make sense for them. This way parents have the chance to consider potentially helpful new ideas they may not otherwise have access to, digest and process them, try them out, and consciously integrate the ideas into their parenting styles. This happens best in a community of support, supplemented by written materials such as books, parenting articles, newspaper clips, and so on, all of which serve to reinforce and ground the new material. Parents are seeking information—just peruse the parenting section of the local bookstore, or check into a new moms' "blog." But information that can be received as empowering and non-judgmental (that is, non-prescriptive, sensitive, and conscious) is likely to have the most beneficial impact.

Deeper influences

How do we learn to be parents? We often simply do what was done in our childhoods—to us, for us and around us. Many a parent has repeated the past, for better or for worse. How we were parented lives in us deeply, often unconsciously. Having the chance to unearth memories and raise awareness of how our previous experiences might color current behavior enables parents to see their way toward changing patterns. Selma Fraiberg and her colleagues vividly shine a light on the concept that "in every nursery, there are ghosts. They are the visitors from the unremembered past of the parents, the uninvited guests at the christening."[3] This dark scenario illustrates how the unexplored past can influence the present, particularly during early childhood. Unearthing the influences that live below the surface can only happen with a raised consciousness and remembered feelings. But Alicia Lieberman and colleagues posit that there are also "angels in the nursery," bearing messages of intrinsic goodness, unconditional love and benevolence. These messages, passed from generation to generation, serve as protective shields of parental love, and engender in the child deeply held, early experiences of safety, intimacy, joy and pleasure that foster self worth and healthy emotional integration.[4]

We can be part of a gentle transformative process when we create for parents a non-threatening platform for parents from which they can be encouraged to remember the past and explore the demands of the present, and from which they can see their own struggles within the context of challenges common to all parents.

3   Selma Fraiberg, Edna Adelson and Vivian Shapiro, "Ghosts in the nursery: a psychoanalytic approach to the problems of impaired infant-mother relationships," in *Clinical Studies in Infant Mental Health—the First Year of Life* (London: Travistock Publications, 1980).

4   Alicia Lieberman, Elena Padron, Patricia Van Horn and William W. Harris, "Angels in the Nursery; the Intergenerational Transmission of Benevolent Parental Influences." *Infant Mental Health Journal* (Vol. 26, 2005).

Today's parent

Many parents I encounter today do seem to be looking for help. They are at times lonely, unsure, or stressed. Their relatives may be located too far away to be a regular source of support, or they may wish to be released from family conceptions about child rearing, and therefore have distanced themselves. Mothers are often used to working outside of the home and have a professional identity that evaporates when they take leave to be home with their child.

Mothers are frequently torn. There are financial as well as social insecurities involved with being at home with children. Some mothers cringe inwardly at leaving their children, but find themselves back at work to earn needed income or benefits. Mothers search the Internet, seek out self-help books from the bookstore, and look for other mothers pushing strollers that they can talk to. Despite the plethora of educational resources available to them, they seek *living* support—a community of peers or facilitators to help them navigate the shoals and shallows of parenthood.

But how can we go about providing helpful guidance to parents? How do we share the wisdom of insightful thinkers such as Rudolf Steiner, Emmi Pikler or Magda Gerber without being prescriptive or instilling anxiety over whether or not they are parenting the "right" way? There are, of course, numerous forms of effective parent support, and many paths by which to inform, encourage and validate parents' innate wisdom. Our goal can be to facilitate an informed self confidence. As Nina Barrett confides, "Self confidence is perhaps the most important prerequisite for enjoying motherhood…and the secret is that no one knows the secret: we are each putting our motherhood together from scratch."[5]

One model of parent work

I offer one model that was used as part of a parent-child class I co-taught with Marilyn Pelrine at The Waldorf School in Lexington, Massachusetts. We supplemented the morning classroom experience with two evening meetings for parents per 10-week class. Tuition for the classes included the evening meetings, which covered many topics of family life, such as rhythm, nutrition, media influences, sleep, warmth, creative discipline, play and healthy movement. These evenings were often presented within the context of the seasonal festivals celebrated by our Waldorf community, which reflected Christian, Jewish and other traditions.

Every evening also included elements of *thinking, feeling* and *willing* in a structure akin to that recommended by Steiner for a morning Main Lesson class in a Waldorf school. For example, in December our parent evening focused on Warmth. We explored soul warmth as the human response to the divine gift of Light. We spoke of preparing to celebrate Christmas and Hanukkah, festivals of Light that illumine the darkest, coldest time of the year and through which an exchange of love and warmth occurs between people. We emphasized the inner experience of the gift of light during winter, as well as how to consciously bring warmth to the child's experience, both in terms of physical care and clothing, and in our relationships. We created an opportunity for parents to quietly

---

5 Nina Barrett, *I Wish Someone Had Told Me: A Realistic Guide to Early Motherhood* (Chicago: Academy Chicago Publishers, 1997), p. xiii.

remember seasonal memories and then share them with the larger group, giving everyone the chance to recall his or her own family memories and see them alongside the memories and traditions of others. Then we had the parents work with wool to make a simple angel to bring home, a creature of light created using a medium of warmth. In this instance, we brought in the element of *thinking* through the discussion on the place of warmth during the season of light in the darkness, a chance to explore the *feeling* aspects of past family celebrations, and an experiential or *willing* activity by creating the angel to take home.

In early spring when the bare trees seem forever dead, yet invisibly the sap begins to run and thicken the buds, we spoke of the celebrations of Passover and Easter and their deeper themes of life arising from apparent death. We mentioned how the egg is a symbol common to both celebrations (the Easter eggs and the egg on the Seder plate) and how its crystallized shell contains new life within. At Easter and Passover, the retelling of an important story is essential to the celebration, so we emphasized the theme of storytelling and its value for children. We told them a story so they could experience its impact. We mentioned how telling actual stories from parents' own childhoods, as well as pedagogical stories and little stories to review the day, can deeply satisfy the child and also help move the child from one "place" or mood to another. Parents then paired up to co-create a story they could use at home to help their children move through a sticky part of the day.

Using festivals as an anchor for the parent meetings helped us weave a thread throughout the year and introduce parents to the community and social life of the school. Most importantly, perhaps, we felt that working with the festival content helped connect parents with deep wellsprings of human cultural experience and with the seasonal changes in the natural world, irrespective of their own religious heritage. The three elements of the meetings—stimulating parents' thinking, exploring some feeling aspects in community with other parents, and creating something tangible—seemed to satisfy different people's preferences. It provided an integrating, non-threatening way of framing topics. We used the themes as cornerstones to the evening, and carefully crafted the timing so that the meetings ran efficiently and ended at a reasonable hour.

The trust-building and learning that grew out of the parent evenings helped to strengthen our mornings together with the children. Sharing the adult time made it easier to reach parents more subtly through our modeling during class time with the children. And the fact that families often signed up for subsequent classes created an ongoing familiarity and sense of community among fellow parents and teachers. Many firm friendships among mothers and children grew from those early class times together.

While this approach may not work for every teacher, I offer it as an example of working with parents to accompany and inform their journey while maintaining a respectful attitude of partnership.

How Emmi Pikler worked with families

We may be inspired in this realm, too, by the example of Emmi Pikler. Dr. Pikler began her work as a pediatrician in Hungary in the early part of the last century, advising parents and caring for their children. As a pediatrician, she made weekly home visits to her patients to provide ongoing support to the mothers in her care. Her book, *Peaceful Babies, Contented Mothers*, was written for parents to offer them an approach to childrearing that would nourish both the children and the mothers. Later in her career following World War II, she set up a residential home for orphaned children. This provided her with an opportunity to design and implement an approach to childrearing based on her core beliefs. She was given a building on Lóczy Street in Budapest in which to set up the home, and the Pikler Institute has been affectionately known ever since as "Lóczy." Pikler carefully chose and trained the caregivers who were to carry out her model of care, replacing all the original nurses because she didn't consider them to have the innate delicate sensitivity with the children that she sought. Pikler preferred to hire young women from the countryside who didn't come with the same intellectual and clinical training, but who operated from a more intuitive and gentle stance.

When devising her approach to caring for infants and young children in the orphanage, Pikler was conscious that she did not wish to create conditions that might interfere with the anticipated mother-child bond that would develop once the child was adopted. The caregivers gave exquisite attention to the child during caregiving, but were trained to refrain from extra displays of affection. Dr. Pikler seemed to be able to distill what was required for the creation of a healthy attachment without fostering a dependency in the orphaned child that would one day require painful disengagement. Trainees at the Pikler Institute learn the distinction: "The mother loves the child, so she cares for him. The caregiver [at Lóczy] cares for the child, so she loves him."

The pillars of care at the Pikler Institute are:

- exquisite presence and attention to the child's signals during caregiving, encouraging her active participation;

- ample opportunity for free movement; and

- astute and careful observation.

The success of this approach was validated by a 1972 World Heath Organization study that concluded that adults who spent their early years at Lóczy were as stable and healthy socially, emotionally and in terms of employment as adults who were raised at home.[6]

Pikler made no attempt to educate adoptive parents to continue the practices of the institute. Her aim—through careful, focused caregiving—was to lay the firmest possible foundation for healthy attachment and self-empowerment in the child, but she let adoptive parents supply their own version of affection and permanent upbringing. She recognized that love comes in many languages and flavors, and that by screening the adoptive families she could assure the children a secure home with ongoing parental love that would reinforce the children's basic sense of self esteem and trust that her nurses had carefully fostered. The loving home would fill in the matrix of attachment that had been so carefully and consciously laid down from the first days at Lóczy and reinforced daily by the caregivers. The children had been given enough respect, time, attention and opportunity for self mastery to carry them into their permanent placements unscarred and ready to attach securely to a new set of parents. Emmi Pikler was decades ahead of her time in understanding that parents did not need authoritarian directives; instead she saw that what parents need are informed support and trust in both their innate parenting instincts and in their child's inner developmental sequence and wisdom.

---

6   Ruth Mason, *Respecting Baby: Dr. Emmi Pikler's Philosophy* and *Dr. Pikler's Parenting Concepts* (Los Angeles: Resources for Infant Educarers, 2000).

Conclusion

Enlarging our scope of concern to include the parents of children in our care requires a new set of skills. These skills include sensitivity and courage to bring up all manner of feelings—and they also require a healthy dose of creativity and openness to the unknown. But the underlying motivations that have drawn us to our special work with children impel us to develop these new skills and share our insights. What has motivated us to work with young children has been our compassion for the child's dependent state, our respect for children as sensitive and spiritual beings, and our passionate recognition that the early years are critical to the entire lifetime of the individual. Let us see ourselves as partners with parents—not wiser or more capable, but, rather, having resources to share with them for their parenting journey. By respectfully creating a partnership with parents, our work in service to the young child can have a deeper and more lasting effect.

Bibliography

Coles, Robert, ed. *The Erik Erikson Reader* (New York: Norton Books, 2001).

David, Miraim and Genevieve Appell. *Lóczy, An Unusual Approach to Mothering*, (Paris: Association Pikler-Lóczy for Young Children, 2001).

Gerber, Magda and Allison Johnson. *Your Self-Confident Baby* (New York: John Wiley and Sons, 1998).

Pikler, Emmi, *Peaceful Babies, Contented Mothers*, 1969, reprinted by Sensory Awareness Foundation Bulletin, Mill Valley, CA, no. 14, Winter 1994.

Pikler, Emmi. *Give Me Time*. Translation by Alexandra Sargent of an excerpt from *Lass Mir Zeit* (Munich: Pflaum Verlag, 1988).

Ris, Margaret. "Festivals as Framework: A Model for Parent Education in a Parent-Tot Program." Antioch University thesis, unpublished, 2001.

Steiner, Rudolf. *The Festivals and their Meaning* (London: Anthroposophical Publishing Co., 1957).

Steiner, Rudolf. *The Cycle of the Year as Breathing Process of the Earth* (Hudson, NY: Anthroposophic Press, 1984).

Steiner, Rudolf. *Understanding Young Children: Excerpts from the Lectures of Rudolf Steiner Compiled for the Use of Kindergarten Teachers* (Silver Spring, MD: Waldorf Kindergarten Association of North America, 1994).

Stern, Daniel and Nadia Brunschweiler-Stern. *The Birth of a Mother* (New York: Basic Books, 1997).

ᏧᎣ

Margaret Ris, MEd, taught early childhood classes at the Waldorf School, Lexington, Massachusetts, for seventeen years. She has completed advanced training at the Emmi Pikler Institute in Budapest, Hungary, and studies with the Infant Parent Training Institute of the Center for Early Relationship Support at Jewish Family and Children's Services in Waltham, Massachusetts. She has served on the board of directors for Sophia's Hearth Family Center in Keene, NH, for three years and offers parent-child classes at the Cambridge YMCA.

In Praise of Simple Joys

by Carol Nasr Griset

Working with urban families in transition and at risk for homelessness is deeply challenging work. The intense vulnerability of family members experiencing this life situation is almost beyond our imagining. In describing the work I have been developing over the last year and a half, I want to share what I understand as the transformational potential of this work.

The Morning Garden

Our Morning Garden program begins at eight o'clock in downtown Santa Ana, California, when the tall iron gate to a downtown church's courtyard is unlocked and a brightly colored windsock is hung to announce we are open. The mothers begin to arrive with their children and their heavily-laden strollers. Strollers are parked at one end of the courtyard and mothers sit down on a low brick wall or at a patio table to sip a cup of coffee while the children run off to play in the sandbox, on the climbing frame, with wheel toys, sidewalk chalk, or best of all with water. Another session of The Morning Garden has begun! Soon parents and children will go inside to their respective programs.

An interesting mix of personal connections brought The Morning Garden into existence. Father Brad Karelius, the rector of the inner-city Episcopal Church of the Messiah, was a schoolmate of mine from kindergarten through high school. When I read in his church's newsletter that he wished to strengthen the relationship with a nearby emergency shelter that housed homeless families, I had the inspiration to begin the parent-child morning in February 2007. The program was held in the church's nursery room. Over the next several months it became apparent the program needed to expand to a three-day format. I was able to enlist the enthusiastic help of four friends from my own church, three of whom offered to take on programs designed especially for the parents and one of whom agreed to work with me in the children's playroom. In the fall of 2007, The Morning Garden program for transient families and families experiencing homelessness opened at the church for three days a week: Monday, Tuesday and Wednesday, from 8 to 11 a.m.

The inspiration for the expanded program grew out of the observation that transient families need a place to come when an overnight shelter closes during the day or when motel life wears thin—a place where they can participate in a reliable weekly rhythm, experience respect for the importance of the parent-child bond, and observe active modeling of healthy adult-child interactions. The parents need an alternative to hanging out in the parks or pushing their strollers around the city. The children need a place to call their own where they can relax from the stresses of the street or shelter life and simply be little children. My goal was to offer a calming setting for families, drawing from the insights of Rudolf Steiner, Emmi Pikler, and Magda Gerber for working with young children, while remaining flexible and innovative in meeting the needs of these families. We soon realized that a format with separate programming for adults and children would suit the needs of these families even better than a traditional parent-child program. I envisioned a situation where the babies and children might be in a simple and beautiful playroom while the parents attended a separate program in different rooms of the church.

Initial funding for this vision came as a bequest from a member of Father Brad's church. Subsequently, we were invited to place our program under the umbrella of a daycare center across the street from the church, Hands Together, which adopted our program as a new initiative. Hands Together was able to apply for funding, both public and private, which has allowed us to move forward and has paid our expenses and staff salaries. Although we are still housed in the Episcopal Church of the Messiah, our program does not have a religious affiliation.

As I attempt to distill The Morning Garden experience into words on paper, I think mainly about the attachments we have formed over the last year and a half. I think about how happy we are to see the parents and the children each morning as they come through the gate, and to know that a sense of respect, recognition and trust is developing among us. I think of the mothers who are able to share their stories in a support group while watching a movie together on Mondays, or creating an artistic journal about their hopes and dreams for themselves and their children on Tuesdays. I think of the Wednesday community meal we share around a beautifully laid table complete with dishes, flowers, candles and a tablecloth, a meal that the moms and the cooking coordinator have spent the morning preparing.

There is another set of attachments we form with the children who come into their own space for the morning. Children who came into the playroom with frantic, scattered energy are now able to slow down, relax and play. Children who formerly struggled to sit still at the table for snack now eagerly await the pre-snack hand-washing ritual and then lean forward to have their faces washed. These are the same children who were tense and cautious and pretended boredom and disinterest in earlier days. They are the same children who brought in an attitude of toughness and bravado, who grabbed for food and kicked or threw the toys. Sometimes that still happens, but after a few days of their coming to The Morning Garden, it is easy to see the joy and comfort they radiate as soon as they enter the room. The reliable repetition of our daily events has seeped into their bodies and they know the order of the day, down to the finest detail. They come to feel so confident in the rhythm that they claim the space as theirs. They own it; they are truly at home here!

The children's morning—wash, eat, play

We use food and water as the mainstays of our morning. With buckets of water and paint brushes, we paint the brick walls and columns of the garden courtyard. Many sunny mornings we have washed hands and feet and faces with basins of warm soapy water before entering the room. Once inside the room, our first order of the day is to gather around the table and wash hands with warm cloths and light a candle as we settle in to eat our first snack of the morning. After snack we bring out the basins again, fill them with warm soapy water and wash the dishes and cloths. The children might dip their heads into the water and laugh, or splash each other vigorously. We surrender to the wonders of water—cold water, warm water, soap bubbles, foot baths, squirting water toys and just washing, washing, washing everything in sight from hair to chairs to stairs.

The room is always filled with the good smell of a pot of applesauce with cinnamon or the toasty aroma of brown rice cooking. Wash, eat, play, wash, tidy-up, wash, eat, play…it is a simple and joyful rhythm. We keep the lights low in the room. There are the usual components of a playroom—dollies to tend, puzzles to do, a play kitchen, a rocking boat, a basket of dress-up clothes and hats, and houses to build. There are pull-toys for the toddlers, a barn with animals, a tunnel to crawl through, and wooden boxes that can be a train or a car or a bed. Everybody's favorite adventure seems to be finding cozy places to hide. We do our singing and finger plays at the snack table and the children are slowly building up the ability to listen to a story.

Six months ago, a two-year-old girl would scream in panic whenever the door opened. Now she happily explores the room and plays confidently. She loves to don an apron, wash the dishes, and proudly hang up the clean, wet cloths on the drying rack. A six-year-old boy, formerly tough and withdrawn, now rushes to build a house every day with the big red cloth and wooden clips, shoring up the sides of his house with wooden boxes, and then he delights in lying down inside for a long, quiet rest. A painfully shy and silent three-year-old girl now loves to have her feet washed, lingering in the warm, soapy water and then dried, and massaged with peppermint lotion. I marvel at the possibilities within our little room for healing and transformation.

How does one find words to describe the wonder and delight the children expressed recently when we answered a mysterious knock at our door one morning? On the doorstep we found two dollies wrapped up in a basket with a note that said "We heard there were children here who would take care of these baby dolls. Please give them a good home." An illegible signature was scrawled at the bottom of the page. The older children were captivated by this highly unusual event, and the babies in the basket were immediately adopted and gently carried around for the rest of the morning, and even taken downstairs to join the community meal.

The mothers' morning—filling the well

As the children relax and play, the mothers have gone upstairs for their own programs. If it is a Monday morning, they will be watching movies with someone who has a passion for the power of movies to inspire conversation and self-reflection when watched in a small group. The movies serve as an opportunity for private emotional release or for sharing sadness or good memories with the other mothers in the group. They are hungry to share, to be listened to.

If it is a Tuesday, the mothers are in a parenting support group where they can talk about the struggles they experience being with their children. The medium for relationship here is a craft, sometimes a toy made for their children, sometimes an artistic project, sometimes simply a piece to read together, or a CD to listen to on a parenting topic, such as crying or tantrums or setting limits. Always there is a lighted candle, a snack and an atmosphere of open acceptance for whatever comes up. The mothers have this time of being filled up and supported, experiencing a much-needed break from being with their children all the time.

If it is a Wednesday, the mothers go downstairs into the church's kitchen and help our cook to prepare an amazing feast from scratch, which they will serve to the children. We bring the children downstairs from the playroom at the end of the morning to the parish hall where the parents serve their delicious culinary creations with noticeable pride. We also invite all others who are in the church at the time, which may include staff, clergy, and visitors. It is a real community feast!

For both mothers and children, we strive to create an environment that is calm, reliable, rhythmic, safe, respectful, and homey. Our biggest challenge has been to maintain a steady attendance of participants. Attendance varies widely from day to day. Over the course of the year we have served about twenty families in all, one family attending every day that we have been in session.

Recently, we have started attending a community partnership forum, and word of our program has reached the ears of several other organizations who are interested in the unique way we are approaching families in transition. We are not a typical child care program, stressing literacy or teaching school readiness. Rather, our program stands as a unique antidote to the trauma and anxiety these families experience on a daily basis. We daily witness the deeply transformational potential of the Morning Garden program which gives children and their parents a safe, reliable and nurturing respite for a few hours each week. Members of the larger community have seen this potential, and out of their interest there has arisen a stronger motivation to find additional funding for our program.

In the center of the courtyard garden stands a two-foot high statue of St. Francis holding a dove in his arms. It is elevated on a pedestal, putting his feet at the eye level of an average three-year-old. On the way out, a child will sometimes wave up at this St. Francis, or even reach up to gently kiss the statue's toes. What a gracious way to offer a wordless thank-you for a morning filled with simple joys.

๛

Carol Nasr Griset, a Waldorf early childhood educator for twenty years, has recently become trained in the RIE/Pikler work. She completed her teacher training at the Rudolf Steiner Centre in Toronto, and taught at the Toronto Waldorf School, pioneering the nursery program there in the 1990s. Having completed the Gradalis and LifeWays trainings, her current area of interest is parent education, especially through parent-infant and parent-toddler groups. She recently served on the WECAN mentoring task force and enjoys mentoring in both schools and home-based programs. She is the mother of five grown children and grandmother of two. Carol currently lives in southern California.